Complete Quinoa

Ashley Billey • Wendy Pirk • Jean Paré • James Darcy

HEALTHY COOKING

Cover image: Nutty Quinoa Salad, see page 32

Complete Quinoa

Copyright © Company's Coming Publishing Limited

First Printing February 2014

Library and Archives Canada Cataloguing in Publication

Billey, Ashley, author

Complete quinoa / Ashley Billey, Wendy Pirk, James Darcy, Jean Paré.

(Healthy cooking series)

Includes index.

ISBN 978-1-927126-63-9 (bound)

1. Cooking (Quinoa). 2. Cookbooks. I. Pirk, Wendy, author

II. Darcy, James, author III. Paré, Jean, author IV. Title. V. Series: Healthy

cooking series

TX809.Q55B54 2013   641.6'31   C2013-905697-1

Thanks to Sandy Weatherall of Jinsei Photographics for the food photograpy, to Ashley Billey for recipe prep and food styling, and to Sheridan Maclaren for the recipes on pages 50, 84 and 112; thanks also to Kseniya Ragozina / Photos.com for the photo on page 5 and to ErnestoG / Photos.com for the photo on page 6.

Published by

Company's Coming Publishing Limited

2311 – 96 Street NW

Edmonton, Alberta, Canada T6N 1G3

Tel: 780-450-6223   Fax: 780-450-1857

www.companyscoming.com

We acknowledge the financial support of the Government of Canada through the Canada Book Fund for our publishing activities.

Printed in China

PC: 21

CONTENTS

The Company's Coming Legacy

Jean Paré grew up with an understanding that family, friends and home cooking are the key ingredients for a good life. A busy mother of four, Jean developed a knack for creating quick and easy recipes using everyday ingredients. For 18 years, she operated a successful catering business from her home kitchen in the small prairie town of Vermilion, Alberta, Canada. During that time, she earned a reputation for great food, courteous service and reasonable prices. Steadily increasing demand for her recipes led to the founding of Company's Coming Publishing Limited in 1981.

The first Company's Coming cookbook, *150 Delicious Squares*, was an immediate bestseller. As more titles were introduced, the company quickly earned the distinction of publishing Canada's most popular cookbooks. Company's Coming continues to gain new supporters in Canada, the United States and throughout the world by adhering to Jean's Golden Rule of Cooking: Never share a recipe you wouldn't use yourself. It's an approach that has worked—millions of times over!

A familiar and trusted name in the kitchen, Company's Coming has extended its reach throughout the home with other types of books and products for everyday living.

Though humble about her achievements, Jean Paré is one of North America's most loved and recognized authors. The recipient of many awards, Jean was appointed Member of the Order of Canada, her country's highest lifetime achievement honour.

Today, Jean Paré's influence as founding author, mentor and moral compass is evident in all aspects of the company she founded. Every recipe created and every product produced upholds the family values and work ethic she instilled. Readers the world over will continue to be encouraged and inspired by her legacy for generations to come.

Nutrition Information Guidelines

Each recipe is analyzed using the most current version of the Canadian Nutrient File from Health Canada, which is based on the United States Department of Agriculture (USDA) Nutrient Database.

• If more than one ingredient is listed (such as "butter or hard margarine"), or if a range is given (1 – 2 tsp., 5 – 10 mL), only the first ingredient or first amount is analyzed.

• For meat, poultry and fish, the serving size per person is based on the recommended 4 oz. (113 g) uncooked weight (without bone), which is 2 – 3 oz. (57 – 85 g) cooked weight (without bone)— approximately the size of a deck of playing cards.

• Milk used is 1% M.F. (milk fat), unless otherwise stated.

• Cooking oil used is canola oil, unless otherwise stated.

• Ingredients indicating "sprinkle," "optional," or "for garnish" are not included in the nutrition information.

• The fat in recipes and combination foods can vary greatly depending on the sources and types of fats used in each specific ingredient. For these reasons, the amount of saturated, monounsaturated and polyunsaturated fats may not add up to the total fat content.

Introduction

Quinoa, a member of the goosefoot family and a close relative of both spinach and beets, is an ancient crop that has long been a staple in the Andes of Peru and Ecuador. It is considered a psuedo-cereal, meaning that it is eaten and prepared like a grain even though it is actually a seed. Quinoa thrives in cool, dry temperate regions at high elevations and grows at 10,000 to 20,000 feet above sea level. The Inca were already cultivating quinoa more than 4000 thousand years ago and considered it a sacred crop, but once the Spanish conquistadors rose to power, the practice was forbidden. The super crop was all but forgotten by everyone except Andean peasants, who grew the rugged plants on a small scale to scrape a meagre existence from the harsh Andean landscape.

A few decades ago, quinoa made its way to North America, where it stayed under the radar of the masses but gained popularity among vegetarians and people eating a gluten-free diet.

Recently, with the demand for natural foods on the rise, quinoa's popularity exploded, and the seed was transformed from a food of disdain, eaten only by the poor, to a food of the well-off, much too expensive for the average family to eat on a regular basis. Today, quinoa is much more readily available in the North American market, and the price has come down accordingly.

There has been some concern, however, that the increasing popularity of quinoa in North America is driving up the cost in the South American countries where it is grown, specifically Ecuador, Bolivia, Peru and Columbia, pricing it out of reach of the locals who have used it as a staple for millennia. Fortunately, the plants respond well to the climatic conditions in some regions of Canada and the United States and quinoa is being grown commercially in the Rocky Mountains of Colorado as well as in Alberta, Saskatchewan, Manitoba and Ontario.

Why Eat Quinoa?

Quinoa's main claim to fame is that is a complete protein, an honour usually reserved for animal products, which means that it has all essential amino acids the body needs to remain healthy and function properly. Because it is a complex carbohydrate, quinoa keeps you feeling fuller for longer and does not cause the spike in blood sugar that you find with more refined foods. Quinoa is also highly digestible and naturally gluten free, so it is suitable for any diet.

It is an excellent source of manganese—which helps regulate thyroid function and stabilize blood sugar levels—and is high in fibre, calcium and phospherous, a mineral that is essential in the repair and maintenance of tissues and cells. Quinoa is also a source of folate, which the body requires to produce healthy red blood cells and to repair DNA.

And as if these reasons weren't enough to add quinoa to your diet, this humble little seed is also loaded with anti-oxidants, especially tocopherols, which have known anti-cancer and anti-aging effects.

Another great thing about quinoa is that it is not fussy. It is easy and quick to cook and fits into almost any kind of meal, from breakfast to dessert.

How to Cook Quinoa

Quinoa can be used in the same types of recipes that you would use whole grains such as rice, couscous or barley, but it cooks up in less time than other whole grains, making it the perfect choice for today's busy lifestyle. And it's simple to cook—if you can cook rice, you can cook quinoa.

To start, rinse your seeds (see "To Rinse or Not to Rinse" below) and combine them with cold water in a saucepan. Unless a specific recipe states otherwise, the ratio is 1 cup (250 mL) quinoa to 2 cups (500 mL) water. Make sure you use a pot that is big enough for the amount of quinoa you are cooking (see chart, below). Even though the seeds are tiny, overcrowding them as they cook results in a mushy finished product. Bring the water to a boil, then simmer, covered, over medium-low heat for about 15 minutes. Turn off the heat and let it sit for about 5 minutes before serving. The quinoa will continue to cook as it sits, so the longer you let it sit, the softer it will be. To serve, remove the lid and fluff the quinoa with a fork.

Uncooked quinoa cooks up to almost triple the amount, so if you start with 1 cup (250 mL) of seeds, you'll end up with almost 3 cups (750 mL) of cooked quinoa.

Uncooked Quinoa	Saucepan Size to Use	Yield of Cooked Quinoa
up to 1/2 cups (125 mL)	Small (1 1/2 quart, 1.5 L)	up to 1 1/2 cups (375 mL)
3/4 cup (175 mL)	Medium (2 1/2 quart, 2.5 L)	2 1/4 cups (550 mL)
more than 1 cup (250 mL)	Large (3 1/2 quart, 3.5 L)	more than 3 cups (750 mL)

To Rinse or Not to Rinse?

Quinoa seeds are coated with a substance called saponin, a soapy, bitter film that acts as a natural insecticide and also prevents birds from eating the seeds. Most quinoa sold on the market today is prewashed, but it is still a good idea rinse the seeds before you cook them, just in case a little saponin has lingered. The easiest way to rinse the tiny seeds it to place them in a fine-mesh sieve and hold it under running water. As you wash the seeds, you may see soapy bubbles forming as the saponin is rinsed away.

The Many Faces of Quinoa

Quinoa seeds:

Of the hundreds of different varieties of quinoa that are grown, only a few are commercially available. White quinoa seeds are the most common, but red and black varieties can be found in many well-stocked stores (or on-line). The different coloured seeds can be used interchangeably in recipes and have the same nutritional content. However, white seeds have a somewhat milder flavour than the black or red varieties. With quinoa, the general rule seems to be the darker the colour, the stronger the flavour and the chewier the texture.

Quinoa flour:

Quinoa flour is made from grinding the seeds into a fine powder. You can purchase it in many supermarkets or health food stores, or grind your own at home. It can be used in many baked goods, from cookies and muffins to cakes and pies, and is also excellent for thickening soups, gravies or sauces. Quinoa flour can be substituted for up to half of the all-purpose flour in many recipes and can completely replace wheat flour in others. Because it has no gluten, quinoa flour must be combined with wheat flour in yeast breads.

Quinoa flour contains more protein and fat than wheat flours and therefore does not have as long a shelf life before it goes rancid. Store it in a cool, dry place in a sealed container or in the fridge for about three months. You can also freeze the flour for up to 6 months.

Quinoa flakes:

For quinoa flakes, the seeds are steam-rolled so that they are flattened, much like rolled oats. They can be used in many of the same ways that oats are used, including as a breakfast cereal, as a binder in meatballs or burgers and in baking. Quinoa flakes cook up much quicker than the seeds.

Sprouted quinoa:

Sprouting quinoa allows the seed to germinate, making it more digestible, and increasing the vitamin and mineral content. Sprouting quinoa also enables you to eat the seeds raw, which means you get nutrients that would otherwise be lost in the cooking process. Quinoa sprouts are great in salads and on sandwiches, but can also be substituted for quinoa in many recipes, such as our Chocolate Quinoa Cookies, p. 142)

How to Make Quinoa Sprouts

Makes 1 cup (250 mL)

Place 1/3 cup (60 mL) quinoa and 1 cup (250 mL) water in a shallow dish and let it sit, covered, for about a half an hour. Drain and rinse the quinoa, then place it back in it's dish. Put the cover back on, leaving a small space so that air can circulate. Cover the dish with a cloth to keep dust and other unwelcome visitors out, and let it sit for about 8 hours. Rinse the quinoa again, cover and let sit for another 8 or so hours. Quinoa sprouts can be eaten as soon as the germ uncurls from the seed, so at this point the sprouts should be ready. If you want longer sprouts, rinse them again and let them sit for a few more hours. Short sprouts can be stored in the fridge for up to 2 weeks as long as they were dry to the touch when they were stored, but they taste best when fresh. Longer sprouts have a softer texture than the short ones, and they spoil quickly— they should be eaten within 24 hours.

Salmon Quinoa Lettuce Cups

Makes 18 lettuce cups

Ginger-flavoured salmon nestled in delicate lettuce leaves—we don't call them appetizers for nothing!

1 cup (250 mL) cooked quinoa

1 x 6 oz (170 g) can of skinless, boneless pink salmon, drained

1/4 cup (60 mL) orange juice

1 Tbsp (15 mL) liquid honey

1 tsp (5 mL) soy sauce

1/2 tsp (2 mL) dry mustard

1/2 tsp (2 mL) finely grated ginger root

1/2 tsp (2 mL) sesame oil

18 small butter lettuce leaves

1 Tbsp (15 mL) sesame seeds, toasted (see Tip)

Toss quinoa and salmon together in a medium bowl.

Combine next 6 ingredients in a small bowl. Add to quinoa mixture and stir until coated. Chill for about 1 hour until cold.

Arrange lettuce leaves in a single layer on a large serving platter. Place about 1 Tbsp (15 mL) quinoa mixture in centre of each leaf. Sprinkle with sesame seeds.

1 lettuce cup: 58 Calories; 1.3 g Total Fat (0.3 g Mono, 0.4 g Poly, 0.1 g Sat); 7 mg Cholesterol; 8 g Carbohydrate; 1 g Fibre; 4 g Protein; 64 mg Sodium

Tip

When toasting nuts, seeds or coconut, cooking times will vary for each type of nut—so never toast them together. For small amounts, place the ingredient in an ungreased shallow frying pan. Heat on medium for 3 to 5 minutes, stirring often, until golden. For larger amounts, spread the ingredient evenly in an ungreased shallow pan. Bake in a 350°F (175°C) oven for 5 to 10 minutes, stirring or shaking often, until golden.

Stuffed Mushrooms

Makes 24 stuffed mushrooms

Stuffed with mushrooms, bacon, quinoa and cheese, these little beauties will be the hit of the party.

24 fresh large white mushrooms

3 Tbsp (45 mL) olive oil

1 cup (250 mL) finely chopped onion

1/3 cup (75 mL) chopped bacon

2 Tbsp (30 mL) finely chopped celery

1/4 cup (60 mL) prepared chicken broth

1/2 cup (125 mL) cooked quinoa

1 tsp (5 mL) garlic powder

1/2 tsp (2 mL) salt

1/2 tsp (2 mL) pepper

1/4 cup (60 mL) grated Parmesan cheese

1/2 cup (125 ml) grated part-skim mozzarella cheese

3 Tbsp (45 mL) chopped fresh parsley

Remove stems from mushrooms. Finely chop stems and set aside.

Heat oil in a medium frying pan on medium. Add onion, bacon and celery and sauté until onion softens and bacon is starting to get crispy, about 6 minutes.

Stir in reserved mushroom stems and next 5 ingredients and heat through. Remove from heat. Divide filling evenly among mushroom caps and arrange them in a single layer on a greased baking sheet.

Combine Parmesan, mozzarella and parsley. Sprinkle over mushroom caps. Broil on second rack from top for about 5 minutes until heated through. Serve immediately.

1 stuffed mushroom: 52 Calories; 4 g Total Fat (2.5 g Mono, 0 g Poly, 1 g Sat); 4 mg Cholesterol; 2 g Carbohydrate; 1 g Fibre; 2 g Protein; 103 mg Sodium

Red Pepper and Peanut Hummus

Makes 3 3/4 cups (925 mL)

Use roasted red peppers to whip up this vibrantly coloured hummus, which is made with peanut butter instead of the usual tahini and has quinoa for an extra shot of protein.

1 x 19 oz (540 mL) can of chickpeas, rinsed and drained

1 cup (250 mL) chopped roasted red peppers

1/2 cup (125 mL) smooth peanut butter

1/2 cup (125 mL) cooked quinoa

1/4 cup (60 mL) lemon juice

1 tsp (5 mL) ground cumin

1 clove garlic

1/4 tsp (1 mL) ground allspice

1/4 tsp (1 mL) salt

Process all 9 ingredients in a food processor until smooth.

1/4 cup (60 mL): 90 Calories; 5 g Total Fat (0 g Mono, 0 g Poly, 1 g Sat); 0 mg Cholesterol; 9 g Carbohydrate; 2 g Fibre; 4 g Protein; 200 mg Sodium

Quinoa Dolmades

Makes 24 dolmades

Quinoa replaces rice in this update of a Greek classic, upping the protein content and making them truly outstanding!

4 Tbsp (60 mL) olive oil,
divided

1 cup (250 mL) chopped onion

1 clove garlic, minced

3/4 cup (175 mL) quinoa

1/2 cup (125 mL) chopped pine nuts

1 cup (250 mL) prepared chicken broth, *divided*

1/2 cup (125 mL) raisins

3 Tbsp (45 mL) chopped fresh dill

3 Tbsp (45 mL) chopped fresh parsley

2 Tbsp (30 mL) chopped fresh mint

42 grape leaves, rinsed and dried, stem removed, *divided*

1 1/2 Tbsp (25 mL) lemon juice

1/2 cup (125 mL) water

Heat 2 Tbsp (30 mL) olive oil in a medium frying pan on medium. Add onion and garlic, and cook for about 5 minutes, stirring often, until onion starts to soften. Remove from heat.

Stir in quinoa, pine nuts, 1/2 cup (125 mL) broth, raisins, dill, parsley and mint. Set aside.

Cover bottom and sides of a greased 2 quart (2 L) casserole with 10 grape leaves.

Place 24 grape leaves on a work surface, vein side up with the stem side closest to you. Place 1 Tbsp (15 mL) quinoa mixture about 1/2 inch (12 mm) from bottom of leaf. Fold bottom of leaf over quinoa mixture, then fold in sides. Roll leaf up from bottom to enclose filling. Repeat with remaining leaves and quinoa mixture. Arrange rolls seam side down close together over leaves in casserole. Sprinkle with lemon juice and 2 Tbsp (30 mL) olive oil. Cover rolls with remaining grape leaves.

Add remaining 1/2 cup (125 mL) broth and water. Bake, covered, in 350°F (175°C) oven for about 30 minutes, until quinoa is tender.

1 dolmade: 70 Calories; 4 g Total Fat (2.5 g Mono, 1 g Poly, 0 g Sat); 0 mg Cholesterol; 8 g Carbohydrate; 1 g Fibre; 2 g Protein; 25 mg Sodium

Chickpea Spinach Samosas

Makes 40 samosas

Crisp phyllo makes way for a rich filling of chickpeas, spinach and quinoa. Hot curry paste could be used instead of the mild if you'd like to spice it up. Be sure to serve these samosas hot from the oven.

1 Tbsp (15 mL) cooking oil

3/4 cup (175 mL) chopped fennel bulb (white part only)

3/4 cup (175 mL) chopped onion

1 Tbsp (15 mL) mild curry paste

2 tsp (10 mL) finely grated ginger root

1 tsp (5 mL) brown sugar, packed

1/2 tsp (2 mL) ground cumin

2 cloves garlic, minced

1/4 tsp (1 mL) salt

1 x 19 oz (540 mL) can of chickpeas, rinsed and drained

1 1/2 cups (375 mL) chopped fresh spinach leaves, lightly packed

1/2 cup (125 mL) frozen peas

1 cup (250 mL) cooked quinoa

10 phyllo pastry sheets, thawed according to package directions

1/2 cup (125 mL) butter (or hard margarine)

Heat cooking oil in a large frying pan on medium. Add fennel and onion. Cook for about 12 minutes, stirring often, until fennel and onion are starting to brown.

Add next 6 ingredients and cook, stirring, for about 1 minute until fragrant.

Add next 4 ingredients and cook, stirring, for about 3 minutes until spinach is wilted.

Place 1 pastry sheet on your work surface. Cover remaining sheets with a damp towel to prevent them from drying out. Brush sheet with butter and cut it lengthwise into 4 strips. Spoon about 1 Tbsp (15 mL) chickpea mixture along bottom of strip. Fold 1 corner diagonally towards straight edge to form triangle. Continue folding back and forth to enclose filling. Repeat with remaining pastry sheets, butter and chickpea mixture. Arrange on greased baking sheets. Brush with remaining butter. Bake, 1 sheet at a time, in 375°F (190°C) oven for about 15 minutes until golden.

1 samosa: 70 Calories; 3 g Total Fat (1 g Mono, 0 g Poly, 1.5 g Sat); 5 mg Cholesterol; 8 g Carbohydrate; 1 g Fibre; 2 g Protein; 140 mg Sodium

Mushroom Salad Rolls

Makes 6 rolls

A nice light appetizer with Asian flavours and a touch of heat. Quinoa makes an excellent substitute for noodles in these delicate rice paper rolls.

1 tsp (5 mL) cooking oil

1 cup (250 mL) thinly sliced fresh shiitake mushrooms

1 cup (250 mL) thinly sliced oyster mushrooms

3/4 cup (175 mL) cooked red quinoa

1/4 cup (60 mL) finely chopped onion

1/4 cup (60 mL) sliced green onion

2 tsp (10 mL) finely grated ginger root

2 cloves garlic, minced

2 Tbsp (30 mL) hoisin sauce

1 Tbsp (15 mL) lime juice

1 Tbsp (15 mL) soy sauce

1/2 tsp (2 mL) chili paste (sambal oelek)

6 rice paper rounds

6 small butter lettuce leaves

Heat cooking oil in a large frying pan on medium. Add next 7 ingredients and cook for about 5 minutes, stirring occasionally, until mushrooms release their liquid.

Stir in next 4 ingredients and cook, stirring, for about 1 minute. Remove from heat and let stand for 10 minutes.

Place 1 rice paper round in a pie plate or shallow bowl of hot water until just softened. Place on a work surface. Place 1 lettuce leaf on round and spoon about 1/4 cup (60 mL) mushroom mixture over lettuce. Fold sides over filling, then roll up tightly from bottom to enclose filling. Place on a plate and cover with a damp paper towel. Repeat with remaining rounds, lettuce and mushroom mixture.

1 roll: 90 Calories; 1 g Total Fat (0 g Mono, 0.5 g Poly, 0 g Sat); 0 mg Cholesterol; 17 g Carbohydrate; <1g Fibre; 2 g Protein; 330 mg Sodium

Moroccan Lentil Quinoa Soup

Makes about 7 cups (1.75 L)

You'll rock the casbah with this Moroccan-inspired delight. The exotic spices in this vegetarian soup add flavour and a comforting aroma to soft lentils and quinoa.

2 tsp (10 mL) cooking oil

1 cup (250 mL) chopped onion

Heat cooking oil in a large saucepan on medium. Add onion. Cook for 5 to 10 minutes, stirring often, until softened.

2 tsp (10 mL) finely grated ginger root

2 cloves garlic, minced

1 tsp (5 mL) ground turmeric

1 tsp (5 mL) ground cumin

1 tsp (5 mL) ground cinnamon

1 bay leaf

1/8 tsp (0.5 mL) salt

Add next 7 ingredients. Heat and stir for about 1 minute until fragrant.

8 cups (2 L) prepared vegetable or chicken broth

1 cup (250 mL) dried green lentils

1 cup (250 mL) diced carrot

1/2 cup (125 mL) diced celery

1/2 cup (125 mL) quinoa

Add next 5 ingredients. Bring to a boil. Reduce heat to medium-low and simmer, partially covered, for about 1 hour, stirring occasionally. Add quinoa and cook for another 20 minutes, until lentils and quinoa are very soft. Discard bay leaf.

1 Tbsp (15 mL) lemon juice

1 Tbsp (15 mL) chopped fresh cilantro (or parsley)

1 tsp (5 mL) grated lemon zest (see Tip, page 98)

Stir in remaining 3 ingredients.

1 cup (250 mL): 180 Calories; 2.5 g Total Fat (1 g Mono, 1 g Poly, 0 g Sat); 0 mg Cholesterol; 32 g Carbohydrate; 6 g Fibre; 8 g Protein; 720 mg Sodium

Spicy Roasted Red Pepper Soup

Makes about 5 cups (1.25 L)

Versatile for entertaining, this smooth soup with red pepper sweetness and warming chipotle heat can be served hot or chilled. Creamy buttermilk provides the perfect contrast for the smoky, sweet flavours of roasted red pepper.

1 tsp (5 mL) cooking oil	Heat cooking oil in a large saucepan on medium. Add leek and celery, and cook for about 8 minutes, stirring often, until leek is golden and celery starts to soften.
1 cup (250 mL) sliced leek (white part only)	
1/2 cup (125 mL) chopped celery	

1/2 tsp (2 mL) dried basil

1 clove garlic, minced

1/4 tsp (1 mL) salt

1/4 tsp (1 mL) pepper

Add next 4 ingredients and cook, stirring, for about 1 minute until garlic is fragrant.

3 cups (750 mL) prepared chicken broth

1 1/2 cups (375 mL) chopped roasted red pepper

1 1/2 tsp (7 mL) granulated sugar

1/2 tsp (2 mL) finely chopped chipotle peppers in adobo sauce (see Tip)

1 cup (250 mL) cooked quinoa

Stir in next 5 ingredients and bring to a boil. Reduce heat to medium-low and simmer, covered, for about 20 minutes until celery is soft. Carefully process with a hand blender or in a blender until smooth (be sure to follow the manufacturer's instructions for processing hot liquids).

1/2 cup (125 mL) buttermilk

Stir in buttermilk.

Tip

Chipotle chili peppers are smoked jalapeno peppers. Be sure to wash your hands after handling them. Store leftover chipotle chili peppers with their sauce in an airtight container in the refrigerator for up to 1 year.

1 cup (250 mL): 110 Calories; 2.5 g Total Fat (0.5 g Mono, 0 g Poly, 0 g Sat); < 5 mg Cholesterol; 19 g Carbohydrate; 2 g Fibre; 4 g Protein; 670 mg Sodium

Quick Chicken Quinoa Stew

Makes 6 servings

Does waiting around for hours for stew to simmer get you stewing mad? Well, if patience is not your virtue, this is the stew for you. Serve with crusty bread.

2 tsp (10 mL) olive (or cooking) oil

6 boneless, skinless chicken thighs (about 3 oz, 85 g, each)

1 cup (250 mL) chopped celery

1 cup (250 mL) chopped onion

1 cup (250 mL) chopped red pepper

2 cloves garlic, minced

1 x 28 oz (796 mL) can of plum tomatoes (with juice)

2 cups (500 mL) prepared chicken broth

1/4 cup (60 mL) chopped sun-dried tomatoes in oil, blotted dry

3 Tbsp (45 mL) tomato paste (see Tip)

1 tsp (5 mL) dried basil

1/2 tsp (2 mL) dried crushed chilies

1/2 tsp (2 mL) dried oregano

(see next page)

Heat olive oil in a Dutch oven on medium-high. Add chicken and cook, uncovered, for 2 to 3 minutes per side until browned. Transfer to a plate and set aside. Reduce heat to medium.

Add celery and onion to the same pot. Cook for about 5 minutes, stirring often, until onion starts to soften. Add red pepper and garlic. Cook for 1 minute, stirring occasionally.

Stir in next 10 ingredients. Cook for about 5 minutes, stirring occasionally and breaking up tomatoes, until boiling.

Add quinoa and chicken. Reduce heat to medium-low. Simmer, covered, for about 30 minutes until chicken is fully cooked and quinoa is tender.

1 serving: 250 Calories; 7 g Total Fat (3 g Mono, 2 g Poly, 1.5 g Sat); 70 mg Cholesterol; 24 g Carbohydrate; 4 g Fibre; 21 g Protein; 990 mg Sodium

Tip

If a recipe calls for less than an entire can of tomato paste, freeze the unopened can for 30 minutes. Open both ends and push the contents through one end. Slice off only what you need. Freeze the remaining paste in a resealable freezer bag or plastic wrap for future use.

1 tsp (5 mL) salt

1/4 tsp (1 mL) pepper

1/8 tsp (0.5 mL) dried rosemary, crushed

2/3 cup (150 mL) quinoa

Whole Grain Beef Ragout

Makes about 8 cups (2 L)

Ragout is basically French for "stew." But French gourmands may never have envisioned adding grains like quinoa and barley to this simple, yet elegant, delight.

1 Tbsp (15 mL) + 2 tsp (10 mL) canola oil, *divided*

1 lb (454 g) stewing beef, trimmed of fat

1 1/2 cups (375 mL) sliced celery

1 cup (250 mL) chopped onion

1 cup (250 mL) sliced carrot

1 clove garlic, minced

4 cups (1 L) prepared beef broth

1 x 7 1/2 oz (213 mL) can of tomato sauce

1/2 cup (125 mL) pot barley

3 Tbsp (45 mL) chopped sun-dried tomatoes in oil, blotted dry

1/2 tsp (2 mL) dried oregano

1/2 tsp (2 mL) pepper

1/4 tsp (1 mL) dried rosemary, crushed

1/3 cup (75 mL) quinoa

1 Tbsp (15 mL) chopped fresh parsley

1 tsp (5 mL) grated lemon zest

Heat 1 Tbsp (15 mL) canola oil in a large saucepan or Dutch oven on medium-high. Cook beef, in 2 batches, for about 5 minutes, stirring occasionally, until browned on all sides. Transfer to a plate. Reduce heat to medium.

Add 2 tsp (10 mL) canola oil to the same pot. Add next 3 ingredients. Cook, uncovered, for 8 to 10 minutes, stirring often, until onion is golden. Add garlic and cook for 1 to 2 minutes until fragrant, stirring often.

Add next 7 ingredients and beef. Stir, scraping brown bits from the bottom of the pot. Bring to a boil. Reduce heat to medium-low and simmer, covered, for 1 hour, stirring occasionally.

Stir in quinoa. Simmer, covered, for about 30 minutes until barley and quinoa are tender.

Stir in parsley and lemon zest.

1 cup (250 mL): 216 Calories; 8.2 g Total Fat (3.8 g Mono, 1.3 g Poly, 1.9 g Sat); 35 mg Cholesterol; 20 g Carbohydrate; 4 g Fibre; 16 g Protein; 614 mg Sodium

Curried Cauliflower Soup

Makes 5 cups (1.25 L)

This soup has plenty of curry flavour without being overpowering. Very yellow, very chunky and very good.

1 cup (250 mL) chopped onion

1/2 cup (125 mL) diced green pepper

3 cups (750 mL) chopped cauliflower

2 cups (500 mL) water

1 cup (250 mL) light sour cream

1/2 cup (125 mL) milk

1/2 cup (125 mL) mashed potatoes

3/4 cup (175 mL) cooked quinoa

1 Tbsp (15 mL) chicken bouillon powder

2 tsp (10 mL) curry powder

1/4 tsp (1 m) salt

1/8 tsp (0.5 mL) pepper

Cook onion, green pepper and cauliflower in water in a large saucepan or Dutch oven until tender. Do not drain.

Stir in remaining 8 ingredients. Simmer for 2 to 3 minutes to combine flavours.

1 cup (250 mL): 100 Calories; 4 g Total Fat (1 g Mono, 0 g Poly, 2 g Sat); 10 mg Cholesterol; 15 g Carbohydrate; 2 g Fibre; 4 g Protein; 450 mg Sodium

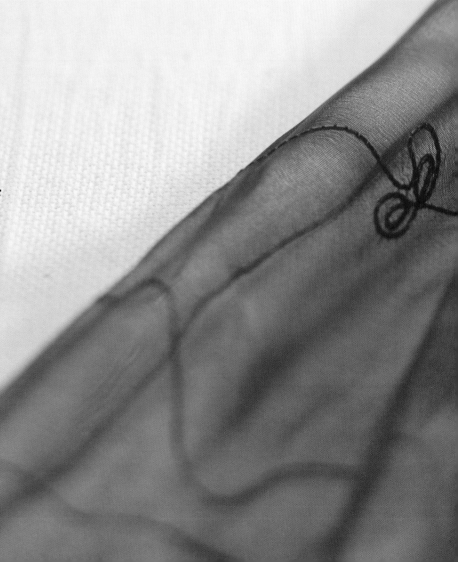

Lemony Chicken and Quinoa Soup

Makes about 9 1/2 cups (2.4 L)

This delightful soup has all the same tangy flavours as lemon chicken.

1 Tbsp (15 mL) cooking oil

3/4 lb (340 g) boneless, skinless chicken breast halves, cut in half lengthwise and cut crosswise into thin strips

1 cup (250 mL) chopped onion

1 cup (250 mL) thinly sliced carrot

1 clove garlic

7 cups (1.75 mL) prepared chicken broth

3/4 cup (175 mL) cup quinoa

1 tsp (5 mL) grated lemon zest (see Tip, page 98)

2 cups (500 mL) fresh spinach leaves, lightly packed, chopped

2 Tbsp (30 mL) lemon juice

Heat cooking oil in a large saucepan on medium-high. Add chicken. Cook for about 4 minutes, stirring often, until no longer pink. With a slotted spoon, transfer chicken to a plate.

Reduce heat to medium. Add next 3 ingredients. Cook for about 10 minutes, scraping any brown bits from the pan, until onion and carrot start to soften.

Add next 4 ingredients. Add chicken. Bring to a boil. Reduce heat to medium-low. Simmer, partially covered, for about 20 minutes, stirring occasionally until quinoa is tender.

Stir in spinach and lemon juice. Cook for about 5 minutes, stirring occasionally, until spinach is wilted.

1 cup (250 mL): 150 Calories; 3 g Total Fat (1.5 g Mono, 1 g Poly, 0 g Sat); 20 mg Cholesterol; 17 g Carbohydrate; 3 g Fibre; 12 g Protein; 760 mg Sodium

Nutty Quinoa Salad

Makes 4 servings

You'll be nutty about this vegetable-packed salad with a zippy dressing. Quinoa is a tasty alternative in salads that usually use couscous or bulgur.

1 1/2 cups (375 mL) water

3/4 cup (175 mL) quinoa

Combine water and quinoa in a medium saucepan. Bring to a boil. Reduce heat to medium-low. Simmer, covered, for about 15 minutes until water is absorbed. Transfer to baking sheet with sides. Spread in thin layer. Chill for 5 to 10 minutes until cool.

1/4 cup (60 mL) chopped red pepper

1/4 cup (60 mL) chopped yellow pepper

1/2 cup (125 mL) halved cherry tomatoes

1/2 cup (125 mL) chopped celery

1/4 cup (60 mL) diced English cucumber

1/4 cup (60 mL) diced zucchini (with peel)

1/4 cup (60 mL) peas, fresh, or frozen, thawed

1/4 cup (60 mL) finely chopped green onion

1/4 cup (60 mL) finely chopped red onion

2 Tbsp (30 mL) chopped fresh oregano

salt to taste

Meanwhile, combine next 11 ingredients in a medium bowl.

For the dressing, whisk all 7 ingredients in a small bowl until combined. Makes about 1/2 cup (125 mL) dressing. Drizzle over salad. Mix in quinoa, and sprinkle with peanuts.

1 serving: 273 Calories; 13.7 g Total Fat (6.3 g Mono, 4.4 g Poly, 2.0 g Sat); 0 mg Cholesterol; 31 g Carbohydrate; 5 g Fibre; 10 g Protein; 256 mg Sodium

3 Tbsp (45 mL) chunky peanut butter

2 Tbsp (30 mL) lime juice

2 Tbsp (30 mL) rice vinegar

2 tsp (10 mL) low-sodium soy sauce

(see next page)

1 clove garlic

2 tsp (10 mL) finely grated
ginger root

1/8 tsp (0.5 mL) cayenne
pepper

1/3 cup (75 mL) chopped
salted peanuts

Avocado Quinoa Salad

Makes about 6 1/2 cups (1.6 L)

A beautiful salad that features protein-rich quinoa, crunchy sunflower seeds, chewy cranberries and creamy avocado. The toasted walnut vinaigrette is a highlight.

1 1/2 cups (375 mL) water

1/4 tsp (1 mL) salt

1 cup (250 mL) quinoa

1 1/2 cups (375 mL) diced avocado

1 cup (250 mL) chopped spinach leaves, lightly packed

1 cup (250 mL) finely chopped fennel bulb (white part only)

1/2 cup (125 mL) chopped dried cranberries

1/4 cup (60 mL) unsalted, roasted sunflower seeds

1 Tbsp (15 mL) chopped fresh chives

1/3 cup (75 mL) walnut pieces, toasted (see Tip, page 9)

1/4 cup (60 mL) olive (or cooking) oil

2 Tbsp (30 mL) lemon juice

1 Tbsp (15 mL) maple syrup

1 tsp (5 mL) dijon mustard

1/2 tsp (2 mL) salt

1/4 tsp (1 mL) pepper

Bring water and salt to a boil in a medium saucepan. Stir in quinoa. Reduce heat to medium-low and cook, covered, for about 20 minutes, without stirring, until quinoa is tender. Remove from heat and let stand, covered, for 5 minutes. Transfer to a large bowl and allow to cool, stirring occasionally, about 20 minutes.

Add next 6 ingredients.

For the dressing, process next 7 ingredients in blender until smooth. Makes about 1/2 cup (125 mL) vinaigrette. Drizzle over quinoa mixture and stir to combine.

1 cup (250 mL): 340 Calories; 21 g Total Fat (10 g Mono, 5 g Poly, 2.5 g Sat); 0 mg Cholesterol; 37 g Carbohydrate; 6 g Fibre; 7 g Protein; 320 mg Sodium

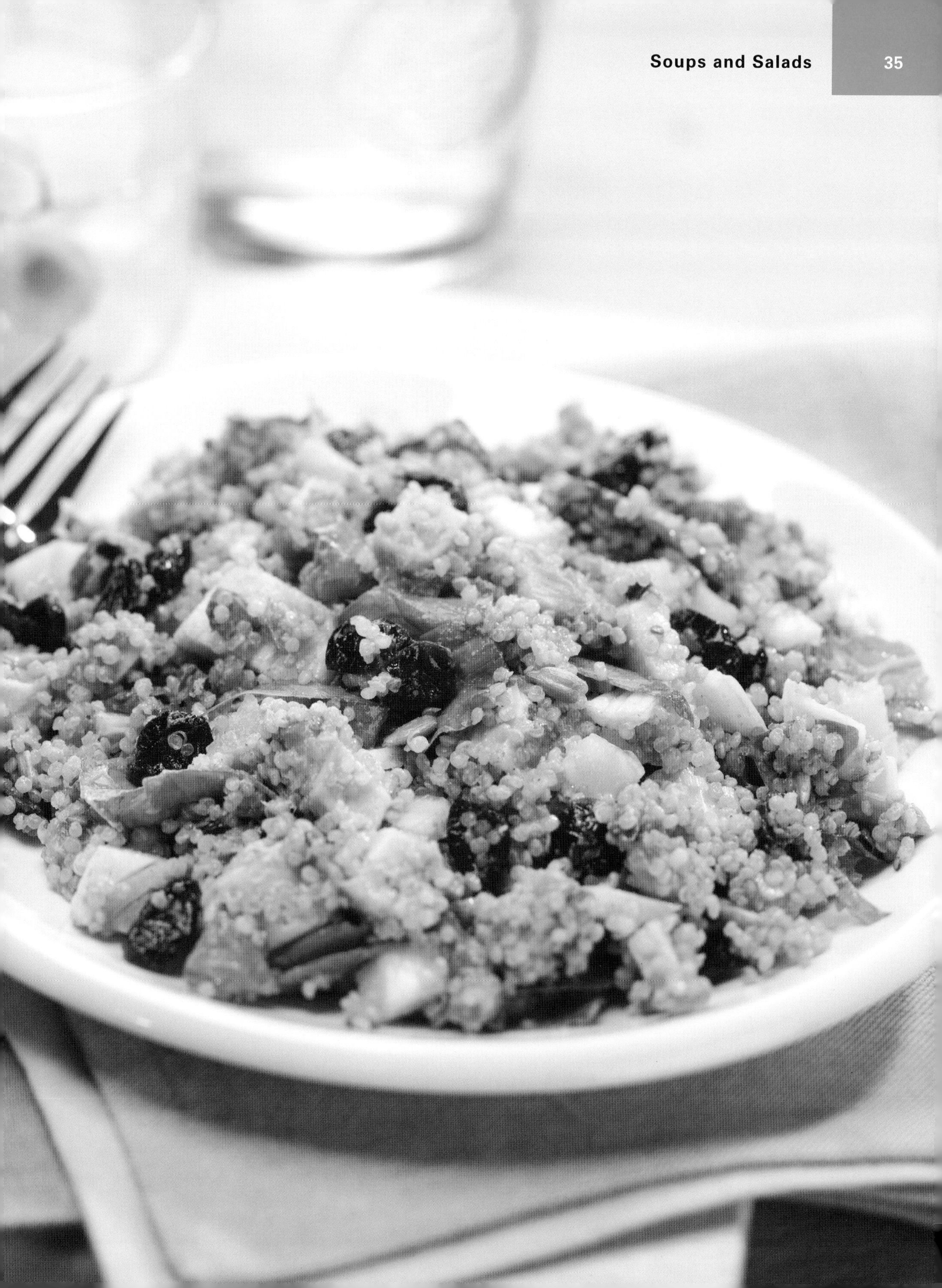

Spinach Tabbouleh

Makes about 4 3/4 cups (1.2 L)

Spinach makes a nice addition to the fresh light flavours of tabbouleh.

2 cups (500 mL) finely chopped fresh spinach leaves

1 cup (250 mL) diced seeded tomato

1/2 cup (125 mL) finely chopped fresh parsley

1/2 cup (125 mL) finely yellow pepper

1/4 cup (60 mL) finely chopped fresh mint

1/4 cup (60 mL) finely chopped green onion

1/4 cup (60 mL) finely chopped radish

1/4 cup (60 mL) lemon juice

2 Tbsp (30 mL) olive oil

1/2 tsp (2 mL) salt

1/4 tsp (1 mL) pepper

1/2 cup (125 mL) cooked quinoa

Combine first 7 ingredients in a large bowl.

Combine next 4 ingredients in a small bowl. Drizzle over spinach mixture and toss to coat. Stir in quinoa.

3/4 cup (175 mL): 90 Calories; 4.5 g Total Fat (3.5 g Mono, 0.5 g Poly, 0.5 g Sat); 0 mg Cholesterol; 10 g Carbohydrate; 3 g Fibre; 3 g Protein; 440 mg Sodium

Blueberry Quinoa Salad

Makes about 6 cups (1.5 L)

This tasty and colourful mix of quinoa and pine nuts is tossed with a fragrant garlic and herb dressing. The unique addition of dried blueberries stands out in fruity bites.

1 1/2 cups (375 mL) water

1/8 tsp (0.5 mL) + 3/4 tsp (4 mL) salt, *divided*

2/3 cup (150 mL) quinoa

2 cups (500 mL) chopped arugula, lightly packed

1 cup (250 mL) canned lentils, rinsed and drained

1/2 cup (125 mL) diced red pepper

1/2 cup (125 mL) dried blueberries

1/4 cup (60 mL) grated Swiss cheese

1/4 cup (60 mL) pine nuts, toasted (see Tip)

2 Tbsp (30 mL) thinly sliced green onion

3 Tbsp (45 mL) olive (or cooking) oil

3 Tbsp (45 mL) raspberry vinegar

1 1/2 tsp (7 mL) lemon juice

3/4 tsp (4 mL) granulated sugar

3/4 tsp (4 mL) pepper

1 clove garlic, minced

Combine water and 1/8 tsp (0.5 mL) salt in a small saucepan. Bring to a boil. Stir in quinoa. Reduce heat to medium-low and simmer, covered, for about 20 minutes, without stirring, until quinoa is tender and liquid is absorbed. Transfer to a large bowl and allow to cool.

Add next 7 ingredients.

Whisk remaining 6 ingredients and 3/4 tsp (4 mL) salt in a small bowl. Add to quinoa mixture and toss until dressing is evenly distributed.

1 cup (250 mL): 275 Calories; 13.6 g Total Fat (6.4 g Mono, 3.4 g Poly, 2.2 g Sat); 6 mg Cholesterol; 30 g Carbohydrate; 7 g Fibre; 8 g Protein; 409 mg Sodium

Tip

Pine nuts have a relatively high oil content and burn easily, so take care when toasting them.

Orange Quinoa Salad

Makes about 6 cups (1.5 L)

Spicy dishes don't have to be overpowering. In this citrusy quinoa salad, spicy chili paste blends perfectly with the flavours of soy, maple and orange for a nicely warming heat.

1/4 cup (60 mL) frozen concentrated orange juice, thawed

2 Tbsp (30 mL) rice vinegar

1 Tbsp (15 mL) low-sodium soy sauce

1 Tbsp (15 mL) maple syrup

1/2 tsp (2 mL) chili paste (sambal oelek)

1/2 tsp (2 mL) garlic powder

1/2 tsp (2 mL) ground ginger

3 cups (750 mL) cooked quinoa

1 cup (250 mL) diced red pepper

1 cup (250 mL) diced yellow pepper

1 cup (250 mL) diced zucchini (with peel)

Whisk first 7 ingredients in a medium bowl until combined.

Toss in remaining 4 ingredients until well combined.

1 cup (250 mL): 365 Calories; 5.1 g Total Fat (1.3 g Mono, 2.1 g Poly, 0.5 g Sat); 0 mg Cholesterol; 70 g Carbohydrate; 7 g Fibre; 12 g Protein; 111 mg Sodium

Spinach Quinoa Salad

Makes about 11 cups (2.75 mL)

The combination of white, red and black quinoa ups this salad's visual appeal, but if you can't find red or black quinoa, just use the white variety.

1/4 cup (60 mL) apple cider vinegar

1/4 cup (60 mL) canola oil

1/4 cup (60 mL) frozen concentrated apple juice, thawed

2 cloves garlic, minced

1/4 tsp (1 mL) ground cinnamon

1/4 tsp (1 mL) ground nutmeg

1/4 tsp (1 mL) salt

1/4 tsp (1 mL) pepper

1 cup (250 mL) cooked quinoa

1 cup (250 mL) cooked red quinoa

1 cup (250 mL) cooked black quinoa

1 cup (250 mL) sliced fresh white mushrooms

1 cup (250 mL) diced unpeeled cooking apple

1/2 cup (125 mL) chopped pecans, toasted (see Tip, page 9)

1/2 cup (125 mL) yellow pepper

4 1/2 cups (1.1 mL) fresh spinach leaves, lightly packed

For the dressing, combine first 8 ingredients in a jar with a tight-fitting lid. Shake well. Makes about 3/4 cup (175 mL) dressing.

For the salad, combine next 7 ingredients in a large bowl. Drizzle dressing over top and toss until mixture is evenly coated. Add spinach and toss lightly.

1 cup (250 mL): 160 Calories; 10 g Total Fat (5 g Mono, 2.5 g Poly, 0.5 g Sat); 0 mg Cholesterol; 17 g Carbohydrate; 3 g Fibre; 3 g Protein; 70 mg Sodium

Japanese Sprout Salad

Makes 12 cups (3 L)

A key ingredient in this exotic salad is Japanese seven-spice blend, also known as *shichimi togarashi*. This spice blend is commonly used in Japanese cooking and generally works well wherever pepper could be used. Japanese seven-spice blend is made of sansho chili peppers, seaweed, chili poppy seeds, shite sesame seeds, black sesame seeds and dried tangerine zest. You can find it in Asian supermarkets.

1/2 medium head of red cabbage

4 1/2 cups (1.1 mL) fresh bean sprouts

2 cups (500 mL) sliced fresh white mushrooms

1/2 cup (125 mL) sliced or slivered almonds, toasted (see Tip, page 9)

1 cup (250 mL) quinoa sprouts (see page 7)

1/4 cup (60 mL) raw sunflower seeds

2 Tbsp (30 mL) sesame seeds

2 green onions, chopped

1/2 cup (125 mL) olive oil

3 Tbsp (45 mL) white vinegar

3 Tbsp (45 mL) soy sauce

1 Tbsp (15 mL) sugar

1 tsp (5 mL) Japanese seven-spice blend

1 tsp (5 mL) salt

1/2 tsp (2 mL) pepper

2 cups (500 mL) dry chow mein noodles

Toss first 8 ingredients together in a large bowl.

For the dressing, place next 7 ingredients in a jar with a tight fitting lid. Shake well. Makes about 3/4 (175 mL) cups dressing. Drizzle over salad and toss well.

Scatter chow mein noodles over top.

1 cup (250 mL): 260 Calories; 16 g Total Fat (9 g Mono, 3 g Poly, 2.5 g Sat); 0 mg Cholesterol; 24 g Carbohydrate; 3 g Fibre; 7 g Protein; 520 mg Sodium

Italian Beef Shells

Makes 4 servings

These pasta shells are filled to the brim with a mildly seasoned beef mixture and topped with crisp golden crumbs.

1 3/4 cups (425 mL) prepared beef broth

1 x 14 oz (398 mL) can of tomato sauce

28 jumbo shell pasta

1 large egg

3/4 cup (175 mL) finely chopped onion

1 x 6 oz (170 mL) jar of marinated artichokes, drained and finely chopped

2/3 cup (150 mL) cooked quino

1/2 cup (125 mL) milk

2 Tbsp (30 mL) chopped fresh basil

1 Tbsp (15 mL) balsamic vinegar

1/2 tsp (2 mL) dried oregano

1 clove garlic

salt and pepper to taste

(see next page)

Combine broth and tomato sauce in 9 x 13 inch (23 x 33 cm) baking dish.

Cook pasta according to package directions, stirring occasionally, until tender but firm. Drain.

Combine next 11 ingredients in a large bowl.

Stir in beef. Spoon about 2 Tbsp (30 mL) beef mixture into each pasta shell. Arrange in a single layer over broth mixture. Cook, covered, in a 350°F (175°C) oven for 1 hour.

Combine crushed crackers and cheese in a small bowl. Sprinkle over shells. Cook, uncovered, for about 15 minutes until crushed crackers are browned and internal temperature of filling reaches 160°F (71°C).

Sprinkle with parsley before serving.

1 serving: 740 Calories; 26 g Total Fat (8 g Mono, 0.5 g Poly, 10 g Sat); 145 mg Cholesterol; 77 g Carbohydrate; 5 g Fibre; 40 g Protein; 2430 mg Sodium

1 lb (454 g) lean ground beef

1 cup (250 mL) crushed round butter-flavoured crackers (about 30)

1/4 cup (60 mL) grated Parmesan cheese

chopped fresh parsley, for garnish

Slow Cooker Stuffed Peppers

Makes 4 stuffed peppers

Tasty and economical, this dish is a complete meal in a pretty little package. Quinoa is a good source of calcium, but you could always sprinkle a little cheese overtop to up the calcium content.

4 large bell peppers, any colour

1 Tbsp (15 mL) cooking oil

1 lb (454 g) lean ground beef

1/4 cup (60 mL) finely chopped onion

3 cloves garlic, minced

1/2 tsp (2 mL) salt

1/4 tsp (1 mL) pepper

1 1/2 cups (375 mL) cooked quinoa

1 x 14 oz (398 mL) can of crushed tomatoes

1 Tbsp (15 mL) finely chopped fresh oregano

1 Tbsp (15 mL) finely chopped fresh basil

2 1/2 cups (625 mL) tomato pasta sauce

Cut a 1/2 inch (12 mm) top from each pepper. Remove seeds and ribs, and trim bottom of each pepper so it sits flat, being careful not to cut into the cavity. Set aside. Remove stems, trimming and dicing any pepper remaining around stems. Discard stems.

Heat a large frying pan on medium. Scramble-fry beef, onion, garlic and diced pepper for about 10 minutes until beef is no longer pink. Sprinkle with salt and pepper, and stir gently. Transfer to a large bowl.

Stir next 4 ingredients into beef mixture. Spoon into prepared peppers. Arrange peppers in a 5 quart (5 L) slow cooker. Pour pasta sauce around peppers. Cook, covered, on Low for 4 to 5 hours or on High for 2 to 2 1/2 hours. Serve peppers with sauce.

1 pepper: 510 Calories: 22 g Total Fat (9 g Mono, 1.5 g Poly, 7 g Sat); 70 mg Cholesterol; 45 g Carbohydrate; 10 g Fibre; 30 g Protein; 1210 mg Sodium

Crispy Mac 'n' Cheese

Makes 6 servings

Classic beefy macaroni and cheese with the added nutrition of carrot and quinoa. Your kids will lick their plates clean.

4 cups (1 L) prepared vegetable broth or water (see Tip)

1/2 cup (125 mL) red quinoa

1/2 tsp (2 mL) salt, *divided*

3 cups (750 mL) elbow macaroni

1/2 lb (225 g) extra-lean ground beef

1 cup (250 mL) diced carrot

1 Tbsp (15 mL) all-purpose flour

1 3/4 cups (425 mL) 2% milk

6 oz (170 g) grated Monterey Jack cheese

1/8 tsp (0.5 mL) ground nutmeg

1 Tbsp (15 mL) lemon juice

5 oz (140 g) grated Cheddar cheese

1/2 cup (125 mL) whole grain bread crumbs or panko (see Tip, page 74)

Preheat oven to 400°F (200°C). Bring vegetable stock to a boil in a large pot. Stir in quinoa and 1/4 tsp (1 mL) salt and cook for 5 minutes before stirring in macaroni. Cover with lid and cook for an additional 7 minutes. When finished, liquid should all be absorbed. Transfer to a large bowl and set aside.

Cook ground beef in a large heavy bottomed pan over high heat until browned. Add carrots and lower heat, cooking for an additional 4 minutes. Remove with rubber spatula and transfer to bowl with pasta. Add flour to pan and gradually whisk in milk until well combined. Adjust heat to medium and allow sauce to heat and thicken. Once sauce has reached a boil, lower heat and stir in Monterey Jack, nutmeg, remaining 1/4 tsp (1 mL) salt and lemon juice. Simmer for another 5 minutes.

Combine sauce, pasta and ground beef in a large bowl. Mix well with a spatula. Pour mixture into a 9 x 15 inch (23 x 33 cm) baking dish. Combine Cheddar cheese and bread crumbs and sprinkle over top.

Bake for 10 minutes, then broil until crispy and golden brown, about 3 minutes. Allow to rest for 4 minutes before serving.

1 serving: 570 Calories; 21 g Total Fat (1 g Mono, 0 g Poly, 12 g Sat); 80 mg Cholesterol; 62 g Carbohydrate; 3 g Fibre; 34 g Protein; 660 mg Sodium

Tip

For a creamier result, add up to 1/4 cup (60 mL) of water. You may need to add more water if you are using a whole grain pasta.

Greek Burgers

Makes 6 burgers

Pita bread replaces the bun in this tempting burger, enlivened with feta, red pepper hummus, sliced tomatoes and fresh spinach.

1/2 cup (125 mL) quinoa

1 cup (250 mL) prepared beef broth

3/4 lbs (340 g) lean ground beef

1/2 cup (125 mL) finely chopped onion

1/2 cup (125 mL) finely chopped red pepper

3 cloves garlic, minced

1/2 tsp (2 mL) ground coriander

1/2 tsp (2 mL) ground cumin

1/4 tsp (1 mL) ground allspice

1 large egg

1/2 cup (125 mL) dry bread crumbs (see Tip, page 74)

1/2 cup (125 mL) feta, crumbled

2 Tbsp (30 mL) chopped fresh oregano

2 Tbsp (30 mL) chopped fresh mint

1/2 tsp (2 mL) salt

1/2 tsp (2 mL) pepper

(see next page)

Rinse quinoa and put into a small sauce pan. Add broth and bring to a boil. As soon as it starts to boil, turn heat down to a simmer and cover. Cook, covered, for about 15 minutes. Remove from heat and fluff with a fork.

Combine next 7 ingredients and quinoa in a large bowl. Add next 7 ingredients and mix thoroughly. Divide quinoa mixture into 6 equal portions and shape into half-moon shape patties, 3/4 inch (2 cm) thick.

Heat grill to medium. Brush patties with oil on each side. Grill the burgers for about 9 minutes per side until internal temperature reaches 160°F (71°C).

Spread hummus over pitas, arranging spinach over one side of hummus and tomato slices over spinach. Place patties over tomatoes. Fold pita over to enclose burger.

1 burger: *450 Calories; 19 g Total Fat (6 g Mono, 1.5 g Poly, 6 g Sat); 80 mg Cholesterol; 42 g Carbohydrate; 5 g Fibre; 22 g Protein; 890 mg Sodium*

1 Tbsp (15 mL) canola oil

6 pita breads

1 cup (250 mL) red pepper hummus

1 cup (250 mL) spinach leaves

1 medium tomato, sliced

Meatloaf with Chipotle Red Pepper Sauce

Makes 8 servings

Comfort food with Southwest flair! Smoked jalapeño peppers add a fiery twist to the sauce.

1 x 12 oz (340 mL) jar of roasted red peppers, drained and chopped

1/4 cup (60 mL) brown sugar, packed

1/4 cup (60 mL) orange juice

3 Tbsp (45 mL) cider vinegar

2 tsp (10 mL) chopped chipotle pepper in adobo sauce (see Tip, page 22)

1/2 tsp (2 mL) salt

1 large egg, fork-beaten

1 cup (250 mL) quinoa flakes

1/4 cup (60 mL) milk

1 Tbsp (15 mL) Montreal steak spice

2 tsp (10 mL) Worcestershire sauce

1 lb (454 g) lean ground beef

1 lb (454 g) lean ground pork

Combine first 6 ingredients in a saucepan. Bring to a boil. Simmer, partially covered, on medium-low for 15 minutes to blend flavours. In a blender or food processor, carefully process until smooth (be sure to follow manufacturer's instructions for blending hot liquids). Reserve 2/3 cup (150 mL).

Combine remaining 7 ingredients. Form into a 9 x 4 inch (23 x 10 cm) loaf in centre of a greased foil pan. Cook meatloaf on indirect medium heat for 1 hour. Brush with remaining red pepper sauce and cook for about 15 minutes until temperature reaches 160°F (71°C). Cover with foil and let stand for 10 minutes. Cut into 1/2 inch (12 mm) thick slices. Transfer to a serving plate and serve with reserved red pepper sauce.

1 serving: 390 Calories; 21 g Total Fat (3.5 g Mono, 0 g Poly, 7 g Sat); 100 mg Cholesterol; 20 g Carbohydrate; 1 g Fibre; 24 g Protein; 1030 mg Sodium

Pork Fried Quinoa

Makes 4 servings

Quinoa replaces rice in this healthy variation of a Chinese takeout favourite.

2 Tbsp (30 mL) + 1 tsp (5 mL) cooking oil, *divided*

3/4 lb (340 g) pork tenderloin, trimmed of fat and cut into thin strips

2/3 cup (150 mL) chopped onion

2/3 cup (150 mL) chopped celery

2 large eggs

1/8 tsp (0.5 mL) pepper

3 cups (750 mL) cooked quinoa

2 Tbsp (30 mL) soy sauce

2/3 cup (150 mL) peas, fresh, or frozen, thawed

2 green onions, sliced

Heat a wok or large frying pan on medium-high until hot. Add 1 tsp (5 mL) cooking oil. Add pork and stir-fry for about 3 minutes until no longer pink. Transfer to plate and cover to keep warm.

Add 1 Tbsp (15 mL) oil to wok. Once heated, add onion and celery and stir-fry for about 3 minutes until onion starts to brown. Transfer to a small bowl.

Add remaining 1 Tbsp (15 mL) cooking oil to wok. Add eggs and pepper. Break yolks but do not scramble. Cook without stirring for 1 minute. Flip. Immediately start chopping egg with edge of a pancake lifter or spatula until egg is in small pieces and starting to brown.

Add quinoa, pork and soy sauce. Stir-fry for about 2 minutes, breaking up quinoa until it is dry and starting to brown.

Add onion mixture, peas and green onions. Stir-fry for about 1 minute until heated through.

1 serving: 420 Calories; 16 g Total Fat (7 g Mono, 2.5 g Poly, 2 g Sat); 155 mg Cholesterol; 36 g Carbohydrate; 6 g Fibre; 32 g Protein; 590 mg Sodium

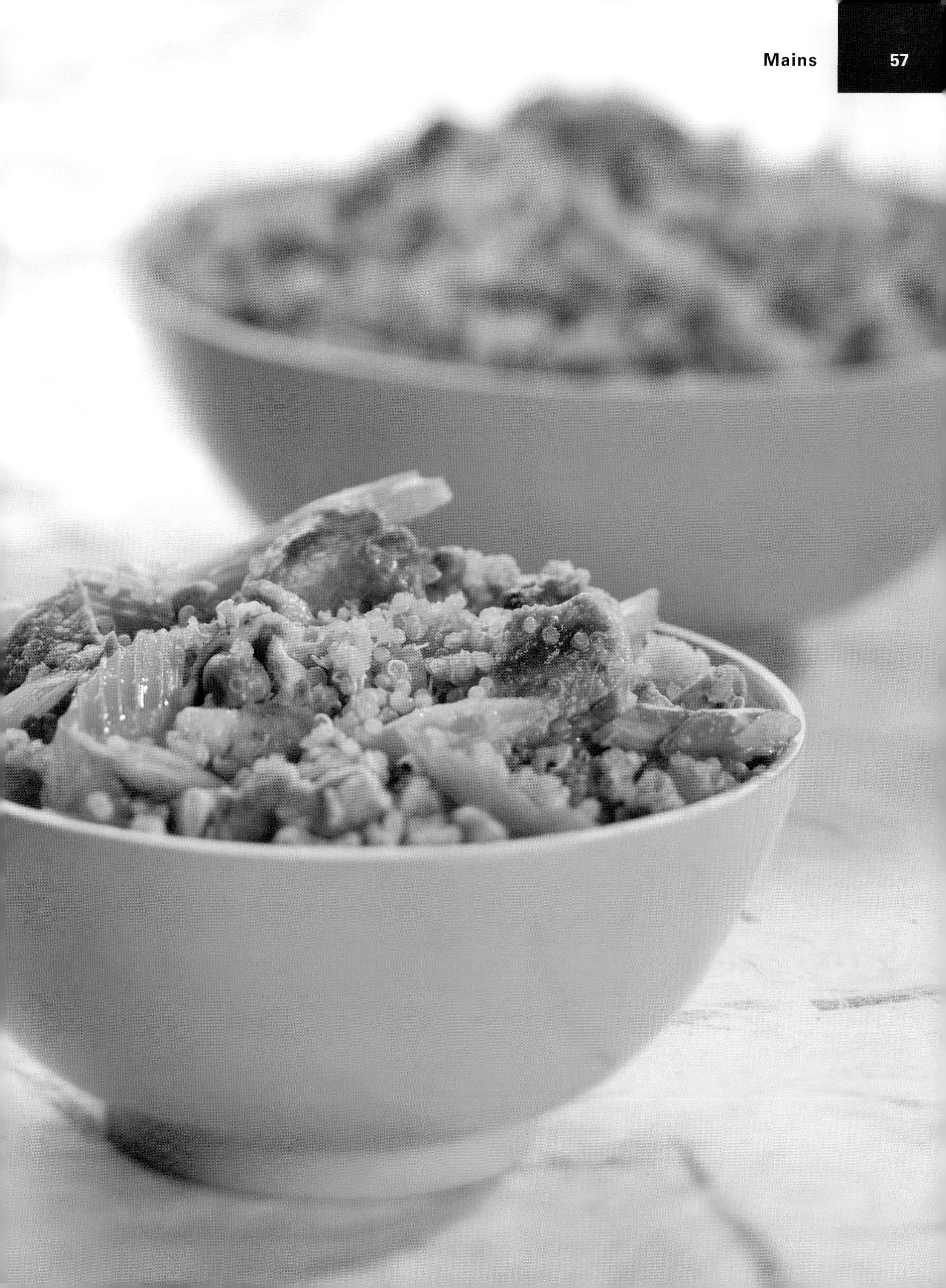

Bavarian Stuffed Pork Roast

Makes 10 servings

Don your lederhosen or dirndl and dig into this tender pork roast stuffed with cabbage, apple and bacon. So good you'll want to yodel!

5 bacon slices, diced

Cook bacon in a large frying pan on medium-high until crisp. Transfer with a slotted spoon to a plate lined with paper towel to drain. Drain and discard all but 1 Tbsp (15 mL) drippings. Reduce heat to medium.

1 1/2 cups (375 mL) shredded green cabbage

1 cup (250 mL) chopped onions

Add next 6 ingredients to same frying pan. Cook for about 8 minutes, stirring often, until onion is soft and starting to brown.

1 cup (250 mL) chopped peeled cooking apples

1 tsp (5 mL) caraway seed

Add vinegar. Heat and stir for 1 minute. Remove from heat. Stir in quinoa, sage and bacon.

1/2 tsp (2 mL) salt

1/4 tsp (1 mL) pepper

Butterfly roast, cutting horizontally lengthwise almost, but not quite, through to other side. Open flat. Place between 2 sheets of plastic wrap. Pound with mallet or rolling pin to 1 inch (2.5 cm) thickness.

1 Tbsp (15 mL) apple cider vinegar

1 1/2 cups (375 mL) cooked quinoa

Spread with mustard. Spoon quinoa mixture over top, leaving 1/2 inch (12 mm) edge. Roll up from 1 long edge to enclose filling. Tie with butcher's string.

2 tsp (10 mL) chopped fresh sage

1 x 3 lb (1.4 kg) boneless centre cut pork roast

Sprinkle with salt and pepper. Place seam side down on greased rack set in medium roasting pan. Cook in 400°F (200°C) oven for 20 minutes. Reduce heat to 325°F (160°C). Cook for about 50 minutes until browned and internal temperature of pork reaches 155°F (68°C). Transfer to a cutting board. Let stand for 10 minutes. Temperature should rise to 160°F (71°C) Remove and discard string. Cut roast into 1/2 inch (12 mm) slices.

1 Tbsp (15 mL) dijon mustard

salt and pepper to taste

1 serving: 300 Calories; 17 g Total Fat (3.5 g Mono, 1 g Poly, 8 g Sat); 80 mg Cholesterol; 10 g Carbohydrate; 1 g Fibre; 28 g Protein; 610 mg Sodium

Lemon Pistachio Pork

Makes 8 servings

Crusted with pepper and stuffed with a sweet dried fruit and pistachio filling, this roast needs little attention once it's on the grill.

1/3 cup (75 mL) liquid honey

3 Tbsp (45 mL) lemon juice

1 Tbsp (15 mL) finely grated lemon zest (see Tip, page 98)

1/2 tsp (2 mL) ground cinnamon

1 cup (250 mL) chopped, roasted pistachios (see Tip, page 9)

1 cup (250 mL) quinoa flakes

1/3 cup (75 mL) dark raisins

1/3 cup (75 mL) dried cranberries

1 x 2 lbs (900 g) boneless pork rib roast, frozen for 30 minutes (see Tip)

2 tsp (10 mL) olive oil

3 Tbsp (45 mL) coarsely ground pepper

1 Tbsp (15 mL) smoked sweet pepper

1 1/2 tsp (7 mL) seasoned salt

Combine first 4 ingredients.

Add next 4 ingredients and stir until combined.

Place roast, fat side up, on a cutting board. Using a sharp knife, cut horizontally, about 1/2 inch (12 mm) from bottom, almost but not quite through to other side. Repeat , if necessary, until roast is an even 1/2 inch (12 mm) thickness. Spread pistachio mixture over roast, leaving a 1/2 inch (12 mm) border. Roll up tightly from short edge to enclose. Tie with butcher's string at 1 inch (2.5 cm) intervals.

Brush entire surface of roast with olive oil. Combine remaining 3 ingredients and sprinkle over roast. Prepare grill for indirect medium heat with a drip pan. Cook roast, fat side up, for about 1 1/2 hours, turning once, until internal temperature of pork reaches at least 140°F (60°C) or until desired doneness. Cover with foil and let stand for 15 minutes. Remove string and cut into 1/2 inch (12 mm) thick slices.

1 serving: 410 Calories; 19 g Total Fat (4.5 g Mono, 2 g Poly, 5 g Sat); 60 mg Cholesterol; 36 g Carbohydrate; 4 g Fibre; 26 g Protein; 630 mg Sodium

Tip

Slice your meat more precisely by placing it in the freezer until it is just starting to freeze (approximately 30 minutes). The meat will retain its shape and be quite easy to cut. If you are using meat that is already frozen, let it partially thaw before cutting.

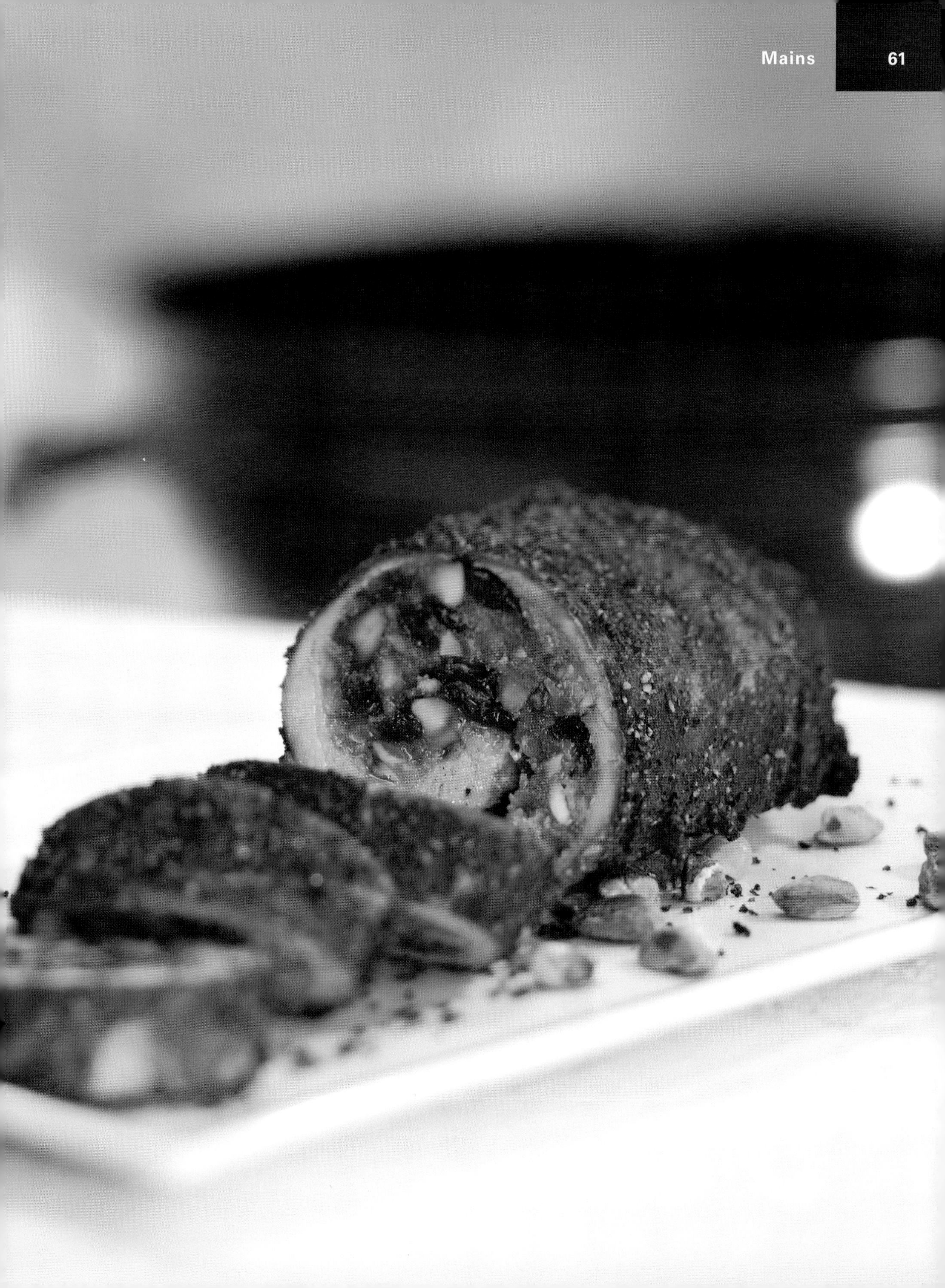

Portobello Pizzas

Makes 4 pizzas

Are your pizzas boring? Perhaps that's because you're still using dough! Portobello caps packed with quinoa and pizza toppings are a new alternative.

4 portobello mushrooms (about 4 inch, 10 cm, diameter), stems and gills removed (see Tip)

1 Tbsp (15 mL) + 2 tsp (10 mL) cooking oil, *divided*

1/4 tsp (1 mL) salt

1/8 tsp (0.5 mL) pepper

1/2 cup (125 mL) finely chopped onion

1/4 cup (60 mL) chopped deli ham

1/2 cup (125 mL) cooked quinoa

3/4 cup (175 mL) grated Swiss cheese, *divided*

1 Tbsp (15 mL) chopped fresh parsley (or 3/4 tsp, 4 mL, flakes)

Brush mushrooms with 1 Tbsp (15 mL) cooking oil. Sprinkle with salt and pepper. Place mushrooms, stem side up, on greased baking sheet.

Heat remaining 2 tsp (10 mL) cooking oil in a large frying pan on medium. Add onion and ham. Cook for about 5 minutes, stirring often, until onion is softened. Remove from heat.

Stir in quinoa, 1/2 cup (125 mL) Swiss cheese and parsley. Spoon into mushroom caps. Cover with greased foil. Bake in 375°F (190°C) oven for 10 minutes. Carefully remove foil. Sprinkle remaining 1/4 cup (60 mL) cheese over top. Bake for about 10 minutes until mushrooms are tender and cheese is melted.

1 pizza: 200 Calories; 12 g Total Fat (4.5 g Mono, 2 g Poly, 4 g Sat); 25 mg Cholesterol; 13 g Carbohydrate; 2 g Fibre; 11 g Protein; 310 mg Sodium

Tip

Because the gills can sometimes be bitter, make sure to remove them from the portobellos. First remove the stems. Then, using a small spoon, scrape out and discard the gills.

Ginger Chicken and Quinoa

Makes about 9 1/2 cups (2.4 L)

A satisfying blend of quinoa and tender chicken. Gentle ginger and colourful vegetables help to brighten it up.

2 tsp (10 mL) cooking oil

2 lbs (900 g) boneless, skinless chicken thighs, trimmed of fat, halved

1 1/2 cups (375 mL) sliced carrot (about 1/2 inch, 12 mm, pieces)

1 1/2 cups (375 mL) sliced leek (white part only), cut in 1/2 inch (12 mm) pieces

1 cup (250 mL) sliced celery

1/2 cup (125 mL) dry (or alcohol-free) white wine

1 1/2 cups (375 mL) prepared chicken broth

1 cup (250 mL) quinoa

1 Tbsp (15 mL) finely grated ginger root

1 clove garlic, minced

1/4 tsp (1 mL) granulated sugar

salt and pepper to taste

1 cup (250 mL) thinly sliced bok choy

1/4 tsp (1 mL) grated orange zest

Heat cooking oil in a large frying pan on medium-high. Add chicken. Cook for about 8 minutes, stirring occasionally, until browned. Transfer with a slotted spoon to 3 1/2 to 4 quart (3.5 to 4 L) slow cooker. Reduce heat to medium.

Add next 3 ingredients to the same frying pan. Cook for about 5 minutes, stirring often, until leek starts to soften. Add wine. Heat and stir, scraping any brown bits from the bottom of the pan, until boiling. Add to slow cooker.

Add next 7 ingredients. Stir. Cook, covered, on Low for 3 to 4 hours or on High for 1 1/2 to 2 hours.

Stir in bok choy and orange zest.

1 cup (250 mL): 251 Calories; 9.5 g Total Fat (3.7 g Mono, 2.5 g Poly, 2.3 g Sat); 63 mg Cholesterol; 18 g Carbohydrate; 2 g Fibre; 21 g Protein; 262 mg Sodium

Chicken Veggie Meatballs

Makes 6 servings

Meatballs are always a favourite with the kids, but these lean morsels have an edge up on the competition: they've got the added flavour and nutritional benefit of fresh veggies and quinoa. A perfect match for spaghetti.

1 large egg, fork-beaten	Combine first 7 ingredients in large bowl.
1/2 cup (125 mL) quinoa flakes	Add chicken and mix well. Roll into 1 inch (2.5 cm) balls. Arrange in a single layer on a greased baking sheet with sides. Broil on oven's top rack for about 7 minutes until no longer pink inside. Makes about 56 meatballs.
1/2 cup (125 mL) grated carrot	
1/2 cup (125 mL) grated zucchini (with peel)	
2 Tbsp (30 mL) grated Parmesan cheese	Bring sauce to a boil in a medium saucepan. Stir in meatballs.
1 tsp (5 mL) Italian seasoning	
1/4 tsp (1 mL) salt	*1 serving:* 260 Calories; 13 g Total Fat (0 g Mono, 0 g Poly, 0.5 g Sat); 95 mg Cholesterol; 19 g Carbohydrate; 4 g Fibre; 18 g Protein; 720 mg Sodium
1 lb (454 g) lean ground chicken	
2 3/4 cups (675 mL) tomato pasta sauce	

Cajun Chicken and Quinoa

Makes about 9 cups (2.25 L)

Try this spicy tomato and quinoa dish and see for yourself what all the fuss is about.

1 1/4 lbs (560 g) boneless, skinless chicken thighs, halved

1 tsp (5 mL) canola oil

1/2 lb (225 g) hot Italian sausage, casing removed, chopped

1 x 14 oz (398 ml) can of diced tomatoes (with juice)

1 1/2 cups (375 mL) chopped green pepper

1 cup (250 mL) chopped celery

1 cup (250 mL) chopped onion

1 cup (250 mL) prepared chicken broth

1 x 7 1/2 oz (213 mL) can of tomato sauce

1/2 cup (125 mL) quinoa

2 tsp (10 mL) Cajun seasoning

2 cloves garlic, minced

Place chicken in a 3 1/2 to 4 quart (3.5 to 4 L) slow cooker.

Heat canola oil in a medium frying pan on medium. Add sausage and scramble-fry for about 5 minutes until starting to brown. Transfer with slotted spoon to a plate lined with paper towel to drain.

Combine remaining 9 ingredients in a large bowl. Pour over chicken. Add sausage and stir well. Cook, covered, on Low for 7 to 8 hours or on High for 3 1/2 to 4 hours until quinoa is tender.

1 cup (250 mL): 220 Calories; 11 g Total Fat (1 g Mono, 1 g Poly, 3.5 g Sat); 70 mg Cholesterol; 11 g Carbohydrate; 2 g Fibre; 19 g Protein; 730 mg Sodium

Chicken Marrakesh

Makes about 5 1/2 cups (1.4 L)

Bring a taste of Morocco to your kitchen with this earthy chicken and quinoa dinner.

1 Tbsp (15 mL) olive oil

1 lb (454 g) boneless, skinless chicken breast halves, cut into 1/4 inch (6 mm) slices

1 tsp (5 mL) salt, *divided*

1/8 tsp (0.5 mL) pepper

1 1/2 cups (375 mL) chopped red pepper

1/4 cup (60 mL) sliced green onion

1 1/2 tsp (7 mL) ground cumin

1/2 tsp (2 mL) ground cinnamon

1/2 tsp (2 mL) ground ginger

1/8 tsp (0.5 mL) cayenne pepper

1 3/4 cups (425 mL) water

1/2 cup (125 mL) dried apricots, chopped

1/2 cup (125 mL) orange juice

1 cup (250 mL) cooked quinoa

1/4 cup (60 mL) sliced almonds, toasted (see Tip, page 9)

Heat a large frying pan or wok on medium-high until very hot. Add olive oil. Add chicken and sprinkle with 1/2 tsp (2 mL) salt and pepper. Stir-fry for about 5 minutes until chicken is no longer pink inside. Transfer to a plate and cover to keep warm.

Add next 6 ingredients and remaining 1/2 tsp (2 mL) salt to the same frying pan. Stir-fry for about 2 minutes until red pepper starts to soften.

Stir in next 3 ingredients and bring to a boil.

Stir in quinoa. Simmer for 5 minutes, then remove from heat and let stand, covered, for 5 minutes. Fluff with a fork. Stir in chicken, and sprinkle with almonds.

1 cup (250 mL): 260 Calories; 7 g Total Fat (4 g Mono, 1 g Poly, 1 g Sat); 55 mg Cholesterol; 23 g Carbohydrate; 4 g Fibre; 25 g Protein; 540 mg Sodium

Baked Spring Rolls

Makes 8 rolls

Just as crisp as the fried variety, with lots of added whole-grain goodness.

1 cup (250 mL) prepared
chicken broth

1/4 cup (60 mL) quinoa

1/4 cup (60 mL) millet

2 tsp (10 mL) + 1 tsp (5 mL)
canola oil, *divided*

1/2 lb (225 g) lean ground
chicken

1 cup (250 mL) finely
chopped onion

1 cup (250 mL) julienned
carrot

1 cup (250 mL) julienned
bamboo shoots

1/2 cup (125 mL) thinly
sliced fresh shiitake
mushrooms

2 Tbsp (30 mL) soy sauce

1 Tbsp (15 mL) finely
grated ginger root

2 cloves garlic, minced

1 tsp (5 mL) chili paste
(sambal oelek)

1 tsp (5 mL) hoisin sauce

16 phyllo pastry sheets,
thawed according to
package directions

Bring broth to a boil in a medium saucepan. Stir in quinoa and millet. Reduce heat to medium-low and simmer, covered, for about 30 minutes, without stirring, until quinoa and millet are tender and broth is absorbed. Transfer to a large bowl and fluff with a fork.

Heat 2 tsp (10 mL) canola oil in a large frying pan on medium-high. Add chicken and scramble-fry for about 5 minutes until no longer pink. Stir into quinoa mixture.

Heat remaining 1 tsp (5 mL) canola oil in same frying pan on medium. Add onion and carrot and cook for about 5 minutes, stirring often, until onion starts to soften.

Add next 7 ingredients and cook, stirring, for about 5 minutes until liquid is evaporated. Add to quinoa mixture.

Place 1 pastry sheet on your work surface with longest side closest to you. Cover remaining sheets with a damp towel to prevent them from drying out. Spray sheet with cooking spray. Place second sheet on top and spray it with cooking spray. Fold in half crosswise and spray with cooking spray. Place about 1/2 cup (125 mL) millet mixture across bottom of sheet, leaving 1 inch (2.5 cm) border on each side. Fold sides over filling. Roll up from bottom to enclose filling. Brush edges with water to seal. Cover rolls with separate damp towel to prevent drying. Repeat with remaining pastry sheets and grain mixture. Spray rolls with cooking spray. Bake in 375°F (190°C) oven for about 25 minutes until browned.

1 spring roll: 303 Calories; 10.1 g Total Fat (3.1 g Mono, 1.7 g Poly, 1.0 g Sat); trace Cholesterol; 41 g Carbohydrate; 3 g Fibre; 12 g Protein; 653 mg Sodium

Salmon Quinoa Frittata

Makes 1 frittatta that cuts into 8 wedges

Don't fritter your time away fretting over dinner. Fix this flavourful frittata and enjoy the finer things in life. Serve with a salad or fresh vegetables.

1 Tbsp (15 mL) canola oil

3/4 lb (340 g) salmon fillet, skin removed, cut into thin strips

7 large eggs

1/4 cup (60 mL) milk

2 Tbsp (30 mL) maple syrup

2 tsp (10 mL) dijon mustard

1/4 tsp (1 mL) salt

1 1/2 cups (375 mL) cooked quinoa

2/3 cup (150 mL) fine dry whole wheat bread crumbs (see Tip)

1/3 cup (75 mL) grated mozzarella cheese

chopped fresh parsley, for garnish

Heat canola oil in a large frying pan on medium. Arrange salmon in single layer in pan.

Whisk next 5 ingredients in a medium bowl until smooth.

Stir in quinoa and bread crumbs. Pour over salmon. Reduce heat to medium-low. Cook, covered, for about 15 minutes until bottom is golden and top is almost set. Remove from heat.

Sprinkle cheese over top. Broil on oven's centre rack for about 5 minutes until cheese is melted and golden. Garnish with parsley.

1 wedge: 239 Calories; 11.0 g Total Fat (4.3 g Mono, 2.4 g Poly, 2.6 g Sat); 190 mg Cholesterol; 17 g Carbohydrate; 1 g Fibre; 18 g Protein; 236 mg Sodium

Tip

To make dry bread crumbs, remove the crusts from slices of stale or two-day-old bread. Leave the bread on the counter for a day or two until it's dry, or, if you're in a hurry, set the bread slices on a baking sheet and bake in a 200°F (95°C) oven, turning occasionally, until dry. Break the bread into pieces and process until crumbs reach the desired fineness. One slice of bread will make about 1/4 cup (60 mL) fine dry bread crumbs. Freeze extra bread crumbs in an airtight container or in a resealable freezer bag.

Jicama Salmon Cakes

Makes 4 cakes

Fishcakes with a facelift—these tasty salmon patties get their great texture from jicama. Zucchini pumps up the veggie factor even more, and quinoa adds a punch of protein. Dill and feta cheese round out the flavours. For an attractive presentation, garnish with tzaziki and pea shoots.

1 cup (250 mL) grated peeled jicama, squeezed dry

1/2 cup (125 mL) grated zucchini (with peel), squeezed dry

1 large egg, fork-beaten

1 x 7 1/2 oz (213 g) can of red salmon, drained, skin and round bones removed

1 cup (250 mL) cooked quinoa

1/4 cup (60 mL) crumbled feta cheese

1/2 tsp (2 mL) dried dillweed

1/4 tsp (1 mL) garlic powder

1/4 tsp (1 mL) salt

1/8 tsp (0.5 mL) pepper

1 Tbsp (15 mL) cooking oil

lemon wedges, for garnish

Combine jicama and zucchini in a large bowl.

Add next 8 ingredients. Mix well. Divide into 4 equal portions. Shape into 3 inch (7.5 cm) patties.

Heat cooking oil in large frying pan on medium. Add patties. Cook for about 5 minutes per side until browned. Serve with lemon wedges.

1 cake: 220 Calories; 11 g Total Fat (3 g Mono, 1 g Poly, 3 g Sat); 80 mg Cholesterol; 19 g Carbohydrate; 6 g Fibre; 12 g Protein; 400 mg Sodium

Quinoa-crusted Tilapia

Makes 4 servings

Toasted quinoa provides a crispy crust for this kid-friendly dish of baked fish and tender veggies. More than one serving of vegetables hides with each serving of fish.

1 Tbsp (15 mL) + 1 tsp (5 mL) cooking oil, *divided*

1/2 cup (125 mL) chopped onion

1 cup (250 mL) chopped fresh (or frozen, thawed) whole green beans

1 cup (250 mL) fresh (or frozen, thawed) kernel corn

1/2 cup (125 mL) chopped red pepper

2 Tbsp (30 mL) Italian dressing

1 large egg

2 Tbsp (30 mL) taco seasoning mix, stirred before measuring

2 Tbsp (30 mL) quinoa, toasted (see Tip)

1 Tbsp (15 mL) all-purpose flour

1 lb (454 g) tilapia fillets, any small bones removed

Heat 1 tsp (5 mL) cooking oil in medium frying pan. Add onion and cook for about 5 minutes, stirring often, until softened.

Add next 3 ingredients. Cook for about 5 minutes, stirring occasionally, until red pepper is tender-crisp.

Add dressing. Cook, stirring, for 1 minute. Remove from heat. Cover to keep warm.

Beat egg with a fork in a medium shallow dish.

Combine next 3 ingredients in separate medium shallow dish.

Dip fillets into egg and press both sides into quinoa mixture until coated. Discard any remaining quinoa mixture.

Heat remaining 1 Tbsp (15 mL) cooking oil in a large frying pan on medium. Add fillets and cook for about 3 minutes per side until golden and fish flakes easily when tested with a fork. Serve fillets with vegetable mixture.

1 serving: 280 Calories; 10 g Total Fat (3.5 g Mono, 1.5 g Poly, 2 g Sat); 115 mg Cholesterol; 18 g Carbohydrate; 2 g Fibre; 27 g Protein; 460 mg Sodium

Tip

Do not rinse quinoa before toasting.

Seafood Quinoa Jambalaya

Makes about 8 cups (2 L)

A nicely textured jambalaya with nutritious quinoa and sweet, tender seafood. The heat is very mild, so add more cayenne pepper if you like things hotter.

2 tsp (10 mL) canola oil

1 1/2 cup (375 mL) chopped onion

1 cup (250 mL) chopped celery

2 Tbsp (30 mL) tomato paste (see Tip, page 25)

2 tsp (10 mL) chili powder

2 cloves garlic, minced

1 tsp (5 mL) dried oregano

1 tsp (5 mL) dried thyme

1/8 tsp (0.5 mL) salt

1/2 tsp (2 mL) pepper

1/4 tsp (1 mL) cayenne pepper

3 cups (750 mL) low-sodium prepared chicken broth, *divided*

1 1/2 cups (375 mL) quinoa

1/2 lb (225 g) small bay scallops

1/2 lb (225 g) uncooked medium shrimp (peeled and deveined)

3/4 cup (175 mL) chopped green pepper

3/4 cup (175 mL) chopped seeded tomato

3/4 cup (175 mL) chopped yellow pepper

Heat canola oil in a large frying pan on medium. Add onion and celery. Cook for about 10 minutes, stirring often, until softened.

Add next 8 ingredients. Heat and stir for about 1 minute until fragrant.

Add 1 cup (250 mL) broth. Heat and stir until boiling. Transfer to 3 1/2 to 4 quart (3.5 to 4 L) slow cooker. Stir in quinoa and remaining 2 cups (500 mL) broth. Cook, covered, on Low for 4 to 5 hours or on High for 2 to 2 1/2 hours.

Stir in remaining 5 ingredients. Cook, covered, on High for about 20 minutes until peppers are tender-crisp and shrimp turn pink.

1 cup (250 mL): 221 Calories; 3.9 g Total Fat (1.3 g Mono, 1.5 g Poly, 0.4 g Sat); 54 mg Cholesterol; 30 g Carbohydrate; 3 g Fibre; 17 g Protein; 373 mg Sodium

Quinoa Chimichurri Casserole

Makes 10 cups (2.5 mL)

A colourful casserole of nutritious quinoa and potatoes, complete with plenty of fresh herbs and a pleasant chili heat that builds.

1 tsp (5 mL) cooking oil

1 cup (250 mL) chopped carrot

1 cup (250 mL) chopped onion

3 cups (750 mL) chopped peeled potato

2 cups (500 mL) prepared vegetable broth

1 cup (250 mL) fresh (or frozen, thawed) kernel corn

1 cup (250 mL) quinoa

1/4 tsp (1 mL) dried crushed chilies

1/4 cup (60 mL) coarsely chopped fresh cilantro

1/4 cup (60 mL) coarsely chopped fresh parsley

2 Tbsp (30 mL) coarsely chopped fresh oregano

(see next page)

Heat cooking oil in a medium frying pan on medium. Add carrot and onion and cook for about 10 minutes, stirring often, until onion is softened. Transfer to greased 3 quart (3 L) casserole.

Stir in next 5 ingredients. Bake, covered, in 375°F (190°C) oven for about 75 minutes until vegetables and quinoa are tender.

Process next 8 ingredients in a blender until smooth. Drizzle over potato mixture.

Stir in red pepper.

1 cup (250 mL): 174 Calories; 4.5 g Total Fat (2.5 g Mono, 1.5 g Poly, 0 g Sat); 0 mg Cholesterol; 30 g Carbohydrate; 4 g Fibre; 5 g Protein; 274 mg Sodium

2 Tbsp (30 mL) cooking oil

1 Tbsp (15 mL) granulated sugar

1 clove garlic, minced

salt and pepper to taste

1 cup (250 mL) finely chopped red pepper

Pasta with Quinoa Red Sauce

Makes 4 servings

Quinoa replaces beef in this vegetarian pasta dish, providing a comparable texture and protein content but without the saturated fat. This sauce also has more fibre and B vitamins than your typical meat sauce. You won't even miss the beef!

8 oz (250g) whole grain pasta

1 Tbsp (15 mL) olive oil

4 cloves garlic, thinly sliced

1/4 cup (60 mL) diced carrots

1/2 cup (125mL) diced celery

1/4 cup (60 mL) diced red onion

1/2 cup (125 mL) fresh tomato

1/2 cup (125 mL) tomato paste (see Tip, page 25)

2 Tbsp (30 mL) red wine vinegar

1/4 tsp (1 mL) salt

1/4 tsp (1 mL) pepper

1 cup (250 mL) prepared vegetable broth or water

1/3 cup (75 mL) red quinoa

2 Tbsp (30 mL) chopped fresh basil

2 Tbsp (30 mL) chopped fresh oregano

4 oz (113 g) shaved Parmesan cheese

Cook pasta according to package directions. Set aside.

Heat oil in a large heavy bottomed pot over medium. Add garlic and cook softly until it becomes fragrant without browning, about 1 minute. Add carrots, celery and onion and cook until vegetables sweat and onion is translucent.

Mix in tomato, tomato paste, vinegar, salt and pepper. Bring sauce to a boil then lower heat and simmer for 10 minutes. Puree sauce with a hand blender until smooth.

Pour vegetable stock and quinoa into sauce. Cover and allow to cook, stirring occasionally, for an additional 15 minutes until quinoa has bloomed. Fold in basil and oregano, and allow to rest for 4 minutes.

To serve, spoon quinoa red sauce over pasta and garnish with Parmesan.

1 serving: 430 Calories; 15 g Total Fat (4.5 g Mono, 0.5 g Poly, 6 g Sat); 20 mg Cholesterol; 55 g Carbohydrate; 12 g Fibre; 22 g Protein; 730 mg Sodium

Mushroom Quinoa

Makes about 5 1/2 cups (1.4 L)

Quinoa, mushrooms and zucchini create an earthy combination of textures. Serve this dish alongside slices of whole wheat baguette paired with olive oil and balsamic vinegar.

1 Tbsp (15 mL) canola oil

3 cups (750 mL) chopped portobello mushrooms

2 cups (500 mL) chopped fresh white mushrooms

2 cups (500 mL) chopped onion

2 cloves garlic, minced

2 Tbsp (30 mL) basil pesto

1 Tbsp (15 mL) + 2 tsp (10 mL) red wine vinegar, *divided*

1/2 tsp (2 mL) pepper

2 cups (500 mL) diced zucchini (with peel)

1 1/2 cups (375 mL) prepared vegetable broth

1 cup (250 mL) quinoa

2 Tbsp (30 mL) grated Parmesan cheese (optional)

Heat canola oil in a large frying pan on medium. Add next 4 ingredients. Cook for about 12 minutes, stirring occasionally, until mushrooms start to brown.

Stir in pesto, 1 Tbsp (15 mL) vinegar and pepper. Transfer to 3 1/2 to 4 quart (3.5 to 4 L) slow cooker.

Stir in next 3 ingredients. Cook, covered, on Low for 4 to 5 hours or on High for 2 to 2 1/2 hours.

Stir in cheese and remaining 2 tsp (10 mL) vinegar.

1 cup (250 mL): 227 Calories; 7.5 g Total Fat (2.0 g Mono, 1.5 g Poly, 0.9 g Sat); 1 mg Cholesterol; 34 g Carbohydrate; 4 g Fibre; 8 g Protein; 191 mg Sodium

Vegetable Quinoa Pie

Makes 1 pie that cuts into 6 pieces

A nutty oat crust holds vegetables and quinoa in a curry-flavoured custard. One bite and this pie is sure to become a favourite.

1 cup (250 mL) + 2 Tbsp (30 mL) all-purpose flour, *divided*

1 1/2 cups (375 mL) quick-cooking rolled oats

1/2 cup (125 mL) butter (or hard margarine), softened

1/2 cup (125 mL) finely chopped unsalted mixed nuts, toasted (see Tip, page 9)

2 Tbsp (30 mL) brown sugar, packed

For the crust, 1 cup (250 mL) flour and next 4 ingredients in a medium bowl until mixture resembles coarse crumbs. Press firmly into the bottom and halfway up the sides of a greased 3 quart (3 L) shallow baking dish. Bake in 350°F (175°C) oven for about 15 minutes until just golden. Let stand on a wire rack to cool.

1 cup (250 mL) prepared vegetable broth

1/8 tsp (0.5 mL) + 1/2 tsp (2 mL) salt, *divided*

2/3 cup (150 mL) quinoa

For the filling, combine broth and 1/8 tsp (0.5 mL) salt in a small saucepan. Bring to a boil. Stir in quinoa. Reduce heat to medium-low. Simmer, covered, for about 20 minutes, without stirring, until quinoa is tender and liquid is absorbed. Fluff with a fork and transfer to a large bowl.

2 tsp (10 mL) cooking oil

3 cups (750 mL) chopped fresh white mushrooms

2 cups (500 mL) chopped onion

2 cloves garlic, minced

Heat cooking oil in a large frying pan on medium. Add next 3 ingredients. Cook for about 10 minutes, stirring often, until onion is softened.

3 cups (750 mL) chopped cauliflower

1 cup (250 mL) chopped red pepper

1 cup (250 mL) grated carrot

Stir in next 3 ingredients. Sprinkle with remaining 2 Tbsp (30 mL) flour, curry powder, remaining 1/2 tsp (2 mL) salt and pepper. Cook, stirring, for 1 minute. Stir into quinoa. Let stand for 10 minutes.

(see next page)

Stir in Gruyère and Cheddar cheese.

Whisk eggs and milk in a medium bowl until combined. Stir into quinoa mixture. Pour into crust and spread evenly. Bake for about 1 hour until knife inserted in centre comes out clean and top is golden. Let stand for 10 minutes.

1 piece: 787 Calories; 43.4 g Total Fat (14.8 g Mono, 4.1 g Poly, 20.1 g Sat); 271 mg Cholesterol; 71 g Carbohydrate; 8 g Fibre; 32 g Protein; 751 mg Sodium

2 tsp (10 mL) curry powder

1/4 tsp (1 mL) pepper

1 cup (250 mL) grated Gruyère cheese

1 cup (250 mL) grated sharp Cheddar cheese

6 large eggs

2 cups (500 mL) milk

Quinoa and Black Bean Burritos

Makes 8 burritos

Use up your leftover quinoa in a dish that can be on the table in less than 15 minutes! The addition of Monterey Jack, avocado and sour cream make for a fine burrito, but use your imagination and personalize your meal—chopped chilies, fresh tomatoes or shredded lettuce would work well.

8 flour tortillas (10 inch, 25 cm, diameter)	Wrap tortillas in foil and place in a 350°F (175°C) oven. Bake for about 10 minutes until heated through.
2 Tbsp (30 mL) cooking oil **1 cup (250 mL) diced red pepper** **1 cup (250 mL) thinly sliced onion** **4 cloves garlic, minced**	Heat oil in a medium frying pan on medium. Add next 3 ingredients and sauté until tender, about 6 or 7 minutes.
1/2 tsp (2 mL) ground cumin **1/4 tsp (1 mL) chili pepper flakes, crushed** **1/4 tsp (1 mL) salt** **1/4 tsp (1 mL) pepper**	Add next 4 ingredients and stir until fragrant. Remove from heat.
1 x 19 oz (540 mL) can of black beans **1 1/2 cups (375 mL) cooked quinoa** **1 cup (250 mL) salsa** **1/2 cup (125 mL) chopped cilantro** **1 avocado, sliced** **1 cup (250 mL) Monterey Jack cheese (optional)** **1/2 cup (125 mL) sour cream (optional)**	Combine next 4 ingredients in a large bowl. Spread tortillas out on a work surface. Divide vegetable mixture down centre of each tortilla, and top with quinoa mixture. Add avocado, cheese and sour cream, if using. Fold sides of each tortilla in and roll up to enclose filling.

1 burrito: 410 Calories; 13 g Total Fat (7 g Mono, 2 g Poly, 2 g Sat); 0 mg Cholesterol; 61 g Carbohydrate; 8 g Fibre; 12 g Protein; 750 mg Sodium

Stuffed Acorn Squash

Makes 4 stuffed squash

A comforting autumn meal that would make a great vegetarian addition to your Thanksgiving spread. Although they look impressive, these little beauties are actually simple to prepare.

4 acorn squash (see Tip)

3 cups (750 mL) cooked quinoa

4 cups (1 L) pumpernickle bread cubes (about 8 slices)

1/2 cup (125 mL) dried cranberries

1/2 cup (125 mL) chopped cashews, toasted (see Tip, page 9)

1/4 cup (60 mL) pumpkin seeds, toasted (see Tip, page 9)

1/4 cup (60 mL) sunflower seeds, toasted (see Tip, page 9)

1 1/2 Tbsp (25 mL) chopped fresh sage

1 Tbsp (15 mL) chopped fresh rosemary

1 Tbsp (15 mL) chopped fresh thyme

(see next page)

Cut 1 1/2 inches (3.8 cm) off top of stem side of each squash and set aside. Remove and discard seeds. Trim bottoms so that each squash will sit flat, being careful not to cut into the cavity. Arrange squash on greased baking sheet with sides.

Combine next 9 ingredients in a large bowl.

Heat butter and oil in a large frying pan on medium. Add next 4 ingredients. Cook for about 8 minutes, stirring often until onion softens.

Stir in vinegar and garlic. Cook for about 1 minute until garlic is fragrant. Add to quinoa mixture. Mix well. Stuff each squash with equal amount of quinoa mixture. Replace stem end. Cook in 400°F (200°C) for about 1 hour, until squash are tender.

1 stuffed squash: 900 Calories; 40 g Total Fat (9 g Mono, 6 g Poly, 11 g Sat); 30 mg Cholesterol; 156 g Carbohydrate; 19 g Fibre; 21 g Protein; 770 mg Sodium

Tip

The aptly named acorn squash resembles an acorn of great proportions. Although more varieties are beginning to emerge, such as golden and white, the most common acorn squash is dark green. It is perfectly normal for a green squash to have orange splotches but you'll want to avoid those that have more orange splotches than green skin. The best squash will be reasonably heavy for its size and have no soft spots.

1/4 cup (60 mL) butter

2 Tbsp (30 mL) cooking oil

1 cup (250 mL) chopped onion

2/3 cup (150 mL) finely chopped celery

1/2 tsp (2 mL) salt

1/2 tsp (2 mL) pepper

1 Tbsp (15 mL) white wine vinegar

1 clove garlic, minced

Pepper Quinoa Pizza

Makes 1 pizza that cuts into 8 wedges

This distinctive, delicious quinoa crust is packed with protein and is gluten free.

1 3/4 cup (425 mL) prepared vegetable broth

1 1/4 cups (300 mL) quinoa

1/4 cup (60 mL) cornstarch

2 Tbsp (30 mL) basil pesto

2 Tbsp (30 mL) canola oil

2 Tbsp (30 mL) yellow cornmeal

1/2 cup (125 mL) tomato sauce

1 cup (250 mL) thinly sliced fresh white mushrooms

1 cup (250 mL) diced red pepper

1 cup (250 mL) diced yellow pepper

3/4 cup (175 mL) grated Asiago cheese

Bring broth to a boil in a medium saucepan. Stir in quinoa. Reduce heat to medium-low and simmer, covered, for about 20 minutes, without stirring, until quinoa is tender and liquid is absorbed. Spread on large plate to cool. Transfer to a food processor.

Add next 3 ingredients. Process until combined and mixture resembles dough.

Sprinkle cornmeal over a well-greased 12 inch (30 cm) pizza pan. Press quinoa mixture into pan. Bake on bottom rack in 450°F (230°C) oven for about 15 minutes until set and edges are dry.

Spread tomato sauce over crust. Scatter remaining 4 ingredients, in order given, over tomato sauce. Bake for about 20 minutes until cheese is melted and golden.

1 wedge: 230 Calories; 12 g Total Fat (2 g Mono, 1 g Poly, 3.5 g Sat); 15 mg Cholesterol; 24 g Carbohydrate; 2 g Fibre; 7 g Protein; 410 mg Sodium

Mushroom Quinoa Burgers

Makes 6 burgers

The days of bland, cardboard-like veggie burgers have past, and we say "Good riddance!" Red quinoa, fresh mushrooms, onion, leek, cashews and feta combine to make a truly sensational pattie that is topped with a garlicky mayonnaise mixture, fresh pea shoots and tomato and cucumber slices.

2/3 cup (150 mL) mayonnaise

3 cloves garlic, crushed

1/2 tsp (2 mL) ground chipolte chili pepper

2 cups (500 mL) water

1/2 tsp (2 mL) salt

1 cup (250 mL) red quinoa, *divided*

1 Tbsp (15 mL) canola oil

3 cups (750 mL) chopped fresh mushrooms

1 cup (250 mL) finely chopped onion

1/4 cup (60 mL) finely chopped celery

1/4 cup (60 mL) finely chopped leek (white part only)

2 cloves garlic

1/2 cup (125 mL) cashews

(see next page)

Combine first 3 ingredients in a small bowl and let it sit for 30 minutes.

Bring water and salt to a boil in medium saucepan. Stir in quinoa and reduce heat to medium-low. Simmer, covered, for about 20 minutes, without stirring, until quinoa is tender and liquid is absorbed. Fluff with a fork and transfer to a large bowl.

Heat canola oil in a large frying pan on medium. Add next 5 ingredients. Cook for about 15 minutes, stirring occasionally, until vegetables start to brown and liquid is evaporated. Remove from heat and cool to room temperature.

Process cashews in a food processor until finely chopped.

Add next 4 ingredients, 1/2 cup (125 mL) quinoa and vegetables. Process with on/off motion until combined. Mixture should still be coarse. Transfer to same large bowl.

Stir in feta and remaining 1/2 cup (125 mL) quinoa. Divide into 6 equal portions and shape into 4 inch (10 cm) patties. Place each patty on greased baking sheet with sides. Spray with cooking spray. Broil on centre rack in oven for about 5 minutes. Turn patties over. Spray with cooking spray and broil for another 5 minutes until brown.

Split each bun in half. Spread mayonnaise mixture on bottom half. Top with the patty, cheese slice, if using, tomato, cucumber, pea shoots and remaining half of bun.

1 burger: 720 Calories; 36 g Total Fat (14 g Mono, 8 g Poly, 7 g Sat); 60 mg Cholesterol; 73 g Carbohydrate; 8 g Fibre; 22 g Protein; 1320 mg Sodium

Tip

Changing the variety of mushroom changes the flavour of your dish. Wild mushrooms have an stronger, earthier flavour than white mushrooms. For this dish, opt for maximum impact and select more flavourful mushrooms. Be experimental and create your own variations by trying different combinations of fresh wild mushrooms. You should find several varieties in your grocery store or produce market.

1 large egg

1 cup (250 mL) fine dry bread crumbs (see Tip, page 74)

1/2 tsp (2 mL) salt

1/2 tsp (2 mL) pepper

3/4 cup (175 mL) feta cheese, crumbled

6 buns

1 medium tomato, sliced

12 cucumber slices

1 cup (250 mL) pea shoots

6 Cheddar cheese slices (optional)

Citrus Spice Quinoa Pilaf

Makes 4 servings

You'll be keen on this fluffy quinoa pilaf scented with lemon and thyme.

2 cups (500 mL) low-sodium prepared chicken broth

1 cup (250 mL) quinoa

1 bay leaf

1 Tbsp (15 mL) olive oil

2 cups (500 mL) diced butternut squash

1 cup (250 mL) chopped onion

2 tsp (10 mL) chopped fresh thyme (or 1/2 tsp, 2 mL, dried)

1/4 tsp (1 mL) dried crushed chilies

salt to taste

2 Tbsp (30 mL) lemon juice

2 tsp (10 mL) grated lemon zest (see Tip)

Combine first 3 ingredients in a medium saucepan. Bring to a boil. Reduce heat to medium-low. Simmer, covered, for about 15 minutes until broth is absorbed. Discard bay leaf.

Meanwhile, heat olive oil in large frying pan on medium. Add next 5 ingredients. Cook, covered, for 5 to 10 minutes, stirring occasionally, until squash and onion are softened and lightly browned. Remove from heat.

Stir in lemon juice, lemon zest and quinoa.

1 serving: 272 Calories; 6.4 g Total Fat (3.3 g Mono, 1.4 g Poly, 0.9 g Sat); 0 mg Cholesterol; 49 g Carbohydrate; 6 g Fibre; 8 g Protein; 33 mg Sodium

Tip

When a recipe calls for both the zest and juice of a citrus fruit, be sure to grate the zest before juicing.

Tunisian Quinoa

Makes about 4 cups (1 L)

If the idea of more rice or potatoes is boring you to tears, don't well up—get cooking. This exotic quinoa pairs with any meat.

1 3/4 cups (425 mL) water

1/4 tsp (1 mL) salt

1 cup (250 mL) quinoa

1 Tbsp (15 mL) olive (or cooking) oil

1 cup (250 mL) chopped onion

1/4 cup (60 mL) finely diced carrot

1/2 cup (125 mL) diced red pepper

1/2 cup (125 mL) frozen peas

1 tsp (5 mL) brown sugar, packed

1/2 tsp (2 mL) ground cumin

1/2 tsp (2 mL) Montreal steak spice

1 clove garlic, minced

1/4 tsp (1 mL) ground cinnamon

1/8 tsp (0.5 mL) cayenne pepper

2 Tbsp (30 mL) lemon juice

Combine water and salt in a small saucepan. Bring to a boil. Stir in quinoa. Remove from heat. Let stand, covered, for 5 minutes. Fluff with a fork. Cover to keep warm.

Meanwhile, heat olive oil in a large frying pan on medium. Add onion and carrot. Cook for about 5 minutes, stirring often, until onion is softened.

Add next 8 ingredients. Cook for about 3 minutes, stirring often, until garlic is fragrant and carrot is tender.

Stir in lemon juice and quinoa.

1/2 cup (125 mL): 120 Calories; 3 g Total Fat (1.5 g Mono, 1 g Poly, 0 g Sat); 0 mg Cholesterol; 19 g Carbohydrate; 3bg Fibre; 4 g Protein; 150 mg Sodium

Roasted Vegetable Quinoa

Makes about 4 cups (1 L)

This light, flavourful Mediterranean-inspired side will have you yearning for the canals of Venice.

1 1/2 cups (375 mL) water

salt to taste

1 cup (250 mL) quinoa

1 cup (250 mL) chopped red pepper

1 cup (250 mL) chopped zucchini (with peel)

1/2 cup (125 mL) chopped onion

3 Tbsp (45 mL) olive (or cooking) oil, *divided*

1/2 tsp (2 mL) dried rosemary, crushed

pepper to taste

10 cherry tomatoes

1 clove garlic clove, minced

3 Tbsp (45 mL) balsamic vinegar

2 Tbsp (30 mL) liquid honey

Preheat oven to 400°F (200°C). Combine water and a sprinkle of salt in a large saucepan. Bring to a boil. Stir in quinoa. Reduce heat to medium-low and simmer, covered, for about 20 minutes, without stirring, until quinoa is tender and liquid is absorbed. Transfer to a medium bowl and fluff with a fork. Cover to keep warm.

Meanwhile, put next 3 ingredients into a medium bowl. Drizzle with 2 Tbsp (30 mL) olive oil. Sprinkle with rosemary, salt and pepper and toss until coated. Spread vegetables in a single layer on a greased baking sheet with sides. Bake for about
15 minutes until starting to brown.

Toss in tomatoes and garlic. Bake for another 5 minutes until tomatoes are hot and vegetables are tender-crisp. Add to quinoa and toss.

Drizzle with remaining 2 ingredients and 1 Tbsp (15 mL) olive oil. Toss until coated.

1/2 cup (125 mL): 161 Calories; 6.4 g Total Fat
(4.1 g Mono, 1.0 g Poly, 0.8 g Sat);
0 mg Cholesterol; 23 g Carbohydrate;
2.4 g Fibre; 3.5 g Protein;
192 mg Sodium

Corn and Quinoa Pilaf

Makes about 5 cups (1.25 L)

The whole grain goodness of quinoa is the star of this healthy, colourful side—sweet corn nicely balances the mild heat. A great side for poultry dishes.

1 1/2 cups (375 mL) prepared vegetable broth

1 cup (250 mL) quinoa

2 tsp (10 mL) cooking oil

1 cup (250 mL) chopped onion

1/2 cup (125 mL) finely chopped kale leaves, lightly packed (see Tip)

1 cup (250 mL) fresh (or frozen, thawed) kernel corn

1/4 cup (60 mL) finely chopped red pepper

2 tsp (10 mL) liquid honey

1 clove garlic, minced

1/2 tsp (2 mL) grated lemon zest

1/2 tsp (2 mL) ground coriander

1/4 tsp (1 mL) ground cumin

1/8 tsp (0.5 mL) salt

1/4 tsp (1 mL) pepper

1/4 cup (60 mL) sliced natural almonds, toasted (see Tip, page 9)

2 Tbsp (30 mL) chopped fresh parsley (or 1 1/2 tsp, 7 mL, dried)

Bring broth to a boil in a medium saucepan. Stir in quinoa. Reduce heat to medium-low. Simmer, covered, for about 20 minutes, without stirring, until quinoa is tender and liquid is absorbed. Fluff with a fork. Transfer to a large bowl. Cover to keep warm.

Heat cooking oil in a large frying pan on medium. Add onion and kale. Cook for about 8 minutes, stirring often, until onion is softened.

Add next 9 ingredients. Cook for about 5 minutes, stirring often, until corn is tender-crisp. Stir mixture into quinoa.

Stir in almonds and parsley.

1 cup (250 mL): 200 Calories; 6 g Total Fat (2.5 g Mono, 1 g Poly, 0 g Sat); 0 mg Cholesterol; 32 g Carbohydrate; 4 g Fibre; 6 g Protein; 250 mg Sodium

Tip

To remove the centre rib from lettuce or kale, fold the leaf in half along the rib and then cut along the length of the rib. To store, place leaves in a large freezer bag. Once frozen, crumble in bag.

Apple Walnut Quinoa

Makes 4 servings

Sweet and spicy, this unusual side dish of toasted walnuts, apples, peppers and irresistibly light quinoa complements almost any entree.

1 1/2 cups (375 mL) prepared vegetable broth

1 cup (250 mL) quinoa

Bring broth to a boil in a medium saucepan. Stir in quinoa. Reduce heat to medium-low and simmer, covered, for about 20 minutes, without stirring, until quinoa is tender and liquid is absorbed.

1 tsp (5 mL) olive oil

1 cup (250 mL) chopped onion

1 clove garlic clove, minced

Heat olive oil in a large frying pan on medium. Add onion and garlic. Cook for 5 to 10 minutes, stirring often, until onion is softened.

1 cup (250 mL) chopped peeled cooking apple (such as McIntosh)

1/2 cup (125 mL) chopped red pepper

2 tsp (10 mL) finely diced fresh hot chili pepper (see Tip)

Add next 3 ingredients. Cook for about 2 minutes, stirring occasionally, until red pepper starts to soften.

1/4 cup (60 mL) chopped walnuts, toasted (see Tip, page 9)

Stir in walnuts and quinoa.

3 Tbsp (45 mL) balsamic vinegar

2 Tbsp (30 mL) liquid honey

1/4 tsp (1 mL) pepper

Combine remaining 3 ingredients in a small cup. Drizzle over quinoa mixture and toss until coated.

1 serving: 311 Calories; 8.8 g Total Fat (2.2 g Mono, 4.7 g Poly, 0.9 g Sat); 0 mg Cholesterol; 52 g Carbohydrate; 6 g Fibre; 8 g Protein; 188 mg Sodium

Tip

Hot peppers contain capsaicin in the seeds and ribs. Removing the seeds and ribs will reduce the heat. Wear rubber gloves when handling hot peppers and avoid touching your eyes. Wash your hands well afterwards.

Quinoa Chickpea Curry

Makes about 5 cups (1.25 L)

Chickpea curries are a tasty staple at Indo-Asian restaurants. We've added nutty quinoa for a one-two punch of nutritious grains and legumes.

1 1/4 cups (300 mL) prepared vegetable broth

1 tsp (5 mL) curry powder

1/4 tsp (1 mL) ground cinnamon

1/4 tsp (1 mL) ground cumin

3/4 cup (175 mL) quinoa

1 tsp (5 mL) cooking oil

1 cup (250 mL) chopped onion

2 cloves garlic, minced

1 x 19 oz (540 mL) can of chickpeas (garbanzo beans), rinsed and drained

1 cup (250 mL) finely chopped red pepper

1/2 tsp (2 mL) salt

1/4 tsp (1 mL) pepper

Combine first 4 ingredients in a small saucepan and bring to a boil. Stir in quinoa. Reduce heat to medium-low. Simmer, covered, for about 20 minutes, without stirring, until quinoa is tender and liquid is absorbed. Fluff with a fork. Cover to keep warm.

Heat cooking oil in medium frying pan on medium. Add onion and garlic. Cook for 5 to 10 minutes, stirring occasionally, until onion is softened.

Add remaining 4 ingredients. Heat and stir for 2 to 4 minutes until red pepper is tender-crisp. Transfer to medium bowl. Add quinoa. Stir.

1 cup (250 mL): 280 Calories; 4.5 g Total Fat (1 g Mono, 1 g Poly, 0.5 g Sat); 0 mg Cholesterol; 49 g Carbohydrate; 10 g Fibre; 13 g Protein; 870 mg Sodium

Hot Chili Quinoa

Makes 4 servings

Healthy quinoa finally comes into its own in this side dish that has it all—sweetness, spice and a texture that can't be beat. Great with grilled chicken or pork.

1 1/2 cups (375 mL) prepared vegetable broth

1 cup (250 mL) quinoa

1 tsp (5 mL) canola oil

1 cup (250 mL) chopped onion

1 clove garlic clove, minced

1/2 cup (125 mL) chopped green pepper

1/2 cup (125 mL) sun-dried tomatoes, softened in boiling water for 10 minutes before chopping

1 Tbsp (15 mL) finely diced fresh hot chili pepper (see Tip, page 106)

3 Tbsp (45 mL) balsamic vinegar

2 Tbsp (30 mL) liquid honey

1/4 tsp (1 mL) pepper

1/4 cup (60 mL) pine nuts, toasted (see Tip, page 38)

Bring broth to a boil in a medium saucepan. Stir in quinoa. Reduce heat to medium-low. Simmer, covered, for about 20 minutes, without stirring, until quinoa is tender and liquid is absorbed. Fluff with a fork and cover to keep warm.

Meanwhile, heat canola oil in a large pan on medium. Add onion and garlic. Cook for 5 to 10 minutes, stirring often, until onion is softened.

Stir in next 3 ingredients. Cook for about 2 minutes, stirring occasionally, until green pepper starts to soften. Add quinoa.

Combine next 3 ingredients in a small cup. Drizzle over quinoa mixture and stir until coated. Sprinkle pine nuts over top.

1 serving: 319 Calories; 9.1 g Total Fat (3.3 g Mono, 3.6 g Poly, 1.2 g Sat); 0 mg Cholesterol; 52 g Carbohydrate; 7 g Fibre; 10 g Protein; 329 mg Sodium

Quinoa Mashed Potatoes

Makes 6 servings

Mashed potatoes never looked so good! Quinoa adds a nutritious kick to the beloved classic.

6 large russet potatoes, quartered

1/2 cup (125 mL) prepared chicken broth

1/2 cup (125 mL) water

1 bay leaf

1/2 cup (125 mL) red quinoa

3/4 cup (175 mL) skim milk

2 Tbsp (30 mL) butter

1/2 tsp (2 mL) salt

1/4 tsp (1 mL) pepper

1/8 tsp (0.5 mL) ground nutmeg

2 tsp (10 mL) lemon juice

Preheat oven to 350°F (175°C). Place quartered potatoes in a large heavy bottomed pot and add cold water until potatoes are submerged. Bring to a boil, then reduce to a simmer and cook for 25 minutes, or until potatoes and tender. Drain cooked potatoes and place on a baking sheet lined with parchment paper. Bake for 5 minutes to dry.

In a medium pot bring chicken broth, water and bay leaf to a boil. Stir in quinoa and simmer until cooked, about 12 minutes. Remove from heat and set aside.

Combine milk, butter, salt, pepper and nutmeg. Bring to a boil. Add potatoes and mash, then whisk aggressively until potatoes are light and fluffy. Fold in cooked quinoa and lemon juice and serve.

1 serving: 320 Calories; 4.5 g Total Fat (1 g Mono, 0 g Poly, 2.5 g Sat); 10 mg Cholesterol; 62 g Carbohydrate; 6 g Fibre; 9 g Protein; 260 mg Sodium

Braised Cabbage Quinoa

Makes 4 servings

The humble cabbage is often overlooked as it sits nestled in amongst the other vegetables in the supermarket, but it shouldn't be. Cabbage is an excellent source of vitamin C and is loaded with polyphenols, which are thought to help protect against cancer. Pair this super-veggie with quinoa and you have a side dish that is a powerhouse of nutrition.

2 cups (500 mL) prepared vegetable broth, *divided*

1/2 cup (125 mL) quinoa

1 Tbsp (15 mL) olive oil

1/2 head green cabbage, quartered, inner leaves removed and shredded

1/2 white onion, sliced

2 tsp (10 mL) flax seed

1/2 tsp (2 mL) fennel seed

1/4 tsp (1 mL) pepper

1 cup (250 mL) dry white wine

1/4 cup (60 mL) white wine vinegar

1/4 tsp (1 mL) salt

1 Tbsp (15 mL) lemon juice

Bring 1 cup (250 mL) broth to a boil in a medium saucepan. Add quinoa, lower heat to medium and cook until liquid is absorbed, about 10 to 12 minutes. Set aside.

Heat oil in a large pot over medium heat. Add cabbage and onion and sauté until vegetables begin to soften, about 3 minutes.

Grind flax, fennel seed and pepper in a small food processor or mortar and pestle. Add spice mixture to cabbage and cook for an additional minute.

Pour in next 4 ingredients and remaining 1 cup (250 mL) stock. Stir well. Cover and cook for about 15 minutes, stirring occasionally. Remove lid and raise the heat to medium-high. Cook until liquid has reduced to a syrupy consistency and coats cabbage well. Remove from heat and allow to rest for 4 minutes. Fold in quinoa and serve.

1 serving: 220 Calories; 5 g Total Fat (3 g Mono, 1.5 g Poly, 0.5 g Sat); 0 mg Cholesterol; 27 g Carbohydrate; 5 g Fibre; 5 g Protein; 470 mg Sodium

Quinoa Stuffing

Makes 8 cups

A great side dish for any home-cooked meal, especially one that involves poultry. Event the kids will love it! Cook your quinoa in broth rather than water and add in herbs or garlic to make it more flavourful.

1 small onion, diced

1/2 cup (125 mL) chopped celery

2 cloves garlic, minced

3/4 cup (175 mL) sliced mushrooms

2 Tbsp (30 mL) butter

1 tsp (5 mL) poultry seasoning

1/2 tsp (2 mL) salt

1/4 tsp (1 mL) black pepper

6 slices dried or lightly toasted bread, cubed (about 4 1/2 cups, 1.1 L)

1/2 cup (125 mL) chopped walnuts or pecans

1 1/2 (375 mL) prepared vegetable broth

3 cups (750 mL) cooked quinoa

In a large skillet, sauté onions, celery and garlic in butter until almost soft. Add mushrooms and heat a few more minutes, until onions are clear and mushrooms are soft.

Add thyme, sage, salt and pepper, stirring quickly just to lightly coat and toast the spices.

Reduce heat to low and add cubed bread and nuts, stirring to combine well. Add vegetable broth until bread is well moistened.

Add quinoa and gently toss to combine well.

Transfer to a 3 quart (3 L) casserole or baking dish, and bake in a 375°F (190°C) for 30 to 35 minutes.

1 cup (250 mL): 260 Calories; 11 g Total Fat (2 g Mono, 4.5 g Poly, 2.5 g Sat); 10 mg Cholesterol; 34 g Carbohydrate; 3 g Fibre; 7 g Protein; 400 mg Sodium

Cinnamon-cardamom Breakfast Quinoa

Makes 4 servings

Savoury quinoa topped with walnuts, raspberries and agave syrup for a touch of sweetness—what better way to start your day?

1/2 cup (125 mL) quinoa

1/2 cup (125 mL) red quinoa

1 cup (250 mL) water

1/2 cup (125 mL) orange juice

3/4 tsp (4 mL) ground cinnamon

4 cardamom pods, crushed

1/4 tsp (1 mL) salt

1/2 cup (125 mL) chopped walnuts

1 cup (250 mL) raspberries

2 Tbsp (30 mL) agave syrup

Drain washed quinoa well in a large fine-mesh sieve.

Combine next 5 ingredients in a heavy medium saucepan. Add quinoa, cover and bring to a boil. Reduce heat to low and cook, covered, until water is absorbed and quinoa is tender, about 20 minutes.

Remove pan from heat and let stand, covered, for 5 minutes. Fluff with a fork. Remove cardamom pods.

Divide quinoa among bowls and top with walnuts, raspberries and agave syrup.

1 serving: 310 Calories; 12 g Total Fat (2 g Mono, 8 g Poly, 1 g Sat); 0 mg Cholesterol; 44 g Carbohydrate; 6 g Fibre; 9 g Protein; 120 mg Sodium

Apple Cinnamon Quinoa

Makes 4 servings

With the flavours of cinnamon and apple, this dish tastes more like a treat than a healthy cereal. Think apple pie for breakfast. Sprinkle finely chopped unpeeled apples overtop for a little burst of colour.

1 cup (250 mL) skim evaporated milk	Combine milk and apple juice in a large saucepan. Heat on medium until hot but not boiling.
1/2 cup (125 mL) apple juice	

Stir in remaining 5 ingredients. Reduce heat to medium-low. Simmer, covered, for 20 to 25 minutes, stirring occasionally, until quinoa is tender.

1 cup (250 mL) quinoa

1/2 cup (125 mL) sweetened applesauce

2 Tbsp (30 mL) brown sugar, packed

1/2 tsp (5 mL) cinnamon

1/8 tsp (0.5 mL) salt

1 serving: 273 Calories; 2.7 g Total Fat (0.7 g Mono, 1.0 g Poly, 0.3 g Sat); 2 mg Cholesterol; 53 g Carbohydrate; 3 g Fibre; 10 g Protein; 161 mg Sodium

Make-ahead Ham and Egg Bake

Makes 8 servings

Simple and convenient, this casserole can be assembled the night before, left to sit in the fridge overnight and then slipped into the oven in the morning. Before long, you have a warm, filling breakfast that will keep you satisfied all morning long.

1 tsp (5 mL) butter

1 loaf bread, sliced

1/2 lb (225 g) diced cooked ham, *divided*

1 1/2 cups (375 mL) chopped green pepper, *divided*

1/2 cup (125 mL) red quinoa, *divided*

3 cups (750 mL) grated Swiss cheese, *divided*

10 eggs

3 1/2 cups (875 mL) milk

2 Tbsp (30 mL) fresh dill, chopped

1/2 tsp (2 mL) pepper

1/4 tsp (1 mL) cayenne pepper

1 tsp (5 mL) red wine vinegar

Lightly grease a 9 x 13 (23 x 33 cm) casserole dish with butter. Line bottom of dish with an even layer of bread. You may have to cut the bread to fit snugly.

For next layer spread half the ham, 3/4 cup (175 mL) green pepper, 1/4 cup (60 mL) quinoa and 1 cup (250 mL) cheese. Repeat sequence, then sprinkle rest of cheese evenly over top.

In a medium bowl whisk eggs and milk. Add dill, pepper, cayenne and vinegar. Pour evenly over contents of dish and cover with plastic wrap. Refrigerate for at least 7 hours or overnight. To cook, preheat oven to 325°F (160°C). Remove plastic wrap and bake dish for 40 minutes. Remove from oven and allow to rest for 5 minutes before serving.

1 serving: 520 Calories; 24 g Total Fat (7 g Mono, 2 g Poly, 11 g Sat); 320 mg Cholesterol; 43 g Carbohydrate; 5 g Fibre; 36 g Protein; 840 mg Sodium

Egg and Pepper Wrap

Makes 4 wraps

This wrap is a cinch to make and is portable—perfect for those morning when you want a warm breakfast but need to run out the door.

1 Tbsp (15 mL) cooking oil

1/4 cup (60 mL) chopped green onion

1/2 cup (125 mL) finely chopped red pepper

1/2 cup (25 mL) finely chopped green pepper

8 large eggs

1/2 cup (125 mL) cooked red quinoa

2 Tbsp (30 mL) milk

1 tsp (5 mL) hot pepper sauce

1/4 tsp (1 mL) salt

1/2 cup (125 mL) salsa

3/4 cup (175 mL) grated medium Cheddar cheese

4 flour tortillas (8 inch, 20 cm, diameter)

Heat cooking oil in a large frying pan on medium. Add next 3 ingredients. Cook for about 5 minutes, stirring often, until peppers are softened.

In a medium bowl, stir next 5 ingredients with a whisk until well combined. Pour into a frying pan. Cook for 2 to 3 minutes, stirring occasionally, until eggs are almost set. Remove from heat. Makes 2 2/3 cups (650 mL) filling.

Spoon salsa and cheese onto each tortilla. Spoon egg mixture down centre of each tortilla. Roll up tightly to enclose filling.

1 wrap: 530 Calories; 26 g Total Fat (6 g Mono, 2.5 g Poly, 9 g Sat); 445 mg Cholesterol; 47 g Carbohydrate; 3 g Fibre; 26 g Protein; 980 mg Sodium

Sesame Chicken Pitas

Makes 4 servings

Chicken, quinoa, lettuce and Mandarin orange segments tucked neatly into a whole wheat pita. The sesame dressing gives it a little Asian flair.

3 Tbsp (45 mL) orange juice

1 Tbsp (15 mL) light mayonnaise

1 Tbsp (15 mL) sesame oil

2 tsp (10 mL) brown sugar, packed

2 tsp (10 mL) finely grated ginger root

1 tsp (5 mL) soy sauce

2 tsp (10 mL) canola oil

1/2 lb (225 g) boneless, skinless chicken breast halves, cut into 1/2 inch (12 mm) strips

2 cups (500 mL) cut or torn leaf lettuce

1 cup (250 mL) cooked red quinoa

2 whole wheat pita breads (7 inch, 18 cm, diameter), halved and opened

1 x 10 oz (284 mL) can of Mandarin orange segments, drained

1/4 cup (60 mL) sliced red onion

1 Tbsp (15 mL) sesame seeds

Combine first 6 ingredients in a small cup. Set aside.

Heat a large frying pan on medium-high until very hot. Add canola oil, then add chicken. Stir-fry for about 5 minutes until no longer pink inside. Transfer to a small bowl. Cover to keep warm.

Put lettuce and quinoa into a medium bowl. Pour half of orange juice mixture over top and toss. Spoon mixture into pita pockets.

Add remaining 3 ingredients to chicken. Pour remaining orange juice mixture over top and toss gently. Spoon into pita pockets.

1 serving: 320 Calories; 11 g Total Fat (3.5 g Mono, 3 g Poly, 1 g Sat); 35 mg Cholesterol; 38 g Carbohydrate; 5 g Fibre; 20 g Protein; 320 mg Sodium

Mango Pancakes

Makes 6 pancakes

With the simple contents of your pantry, exotic breakfasts are at your fingertips. These fluffy pancakes have lots of mango pieces and just the right amount of ginger spice. Try them with maple syrup, garnished with fresh mango and strawberries.

1/2 cup (125 mL)
all-purpose flour

1/2 cup (125 mL) quinoa
flour

1 Tbsp (15 mL) granulated
sugar

1 tsp (5 mL) baking powder

3/4 tsp (4 mL) ground
ginger

1/2 tsp (2 mL) baking soda

1/4 tsp (1 mL) salt

1 large egg

2 cups (500 mL) finely
chopped frozen mango
pieces, thawed, *divided*

1/4 cup (60 mL) milk

2 Tbsp (30 mL) cooking oil

1 Tbsp (15 mL) lime juice

Preheat a griddle to medium-high (see Tip). Combine first 7 ingredients in a large bowl. Make a well in the centre.

Process egg, 1 1/2 cups mango, milk, cooking oil and lime juice in a blender until smooth. Add to well. Add remaining 1/2 cup (125 mL) mango. Stir until just combined. Batter will be lumpy. Spray griddle with cooking spray. Pour batter onto griddle, using 1/3 cup (75 mL) for each pancake. Cook for about 2 minutes until bubbles form on top and edges appear dry. Turn pancake over. Cook for about 2 minutes until bottom is golden. Transfer to a plate. Cover to keep warm. Repeat with remaining batter, spraying griddle with more cooking spray if necessary to prevent sticking.

1 pancake: 180 Calories; 6 g Total Fat (3 g Mono, 1.5 g Poly, 0.5 g Sat); 35 mg Cholesterol; 28 g Carbohydrate; 3 g Fibre; 4 g Protein; 250 mg Sodium

Tip

If you don't have an electric griddle, use a large frying pan. Replace the cooking spray with 1 tsp (5 mL) of cooking oil and heat the pan on medium. Heat more cooking oil with each batch if necessary to prevent sticking.

Multi-grain Pancakes

Makes 10 pancakes

These vanilla and cinnamon-flavoured pancakes pack enough whole-grain goodness to keep you going all morning long.

1/4 cup (60 mL) whole wheat flour

1/2 cup (125 mL) quinoa flour

1/2 cup (125 mL) all-purpose flour

1/4 cup (60 mL) brown sugar, packed

1/4 cup (60 mL) large flake rolled oats

1/4 cup (60 mL) yellow cornmeal

2 tsp (10 mL) baking powder

1 tsp (5 mL) ground cinnamon

1 tsp (5 mL) ground ginger

1/2 tsp (2 mL) baking soda

1/4 tsp (1 mL) salt

1 large egg, fork-beaten

1 1/2 cups (375 mL) buttermilk (or soured milk, see Tip)

2 Tbsp (30 mL) canola oil

1 tsp (5 mL) vanilla extract

Combine first 11 ingredients in a large bowl. Make a well in the centre.

Combine remaining 4 ingredients in a medium bowl. Add to well and stir until just moistened. Batter will be lumpy. Preheat a griddle to medium-high (see Tip, 128). Reduce heat to medium. Spray with cooking spray. Pour batter onto griddle, using about 1/3 cup (75 mL) for each pancake. Cook for about 2 minutes until bubbles form on top and edges appear dry. Turn pancake over. Cook for about 2 minutes until browned. Transfer to a plate and cover to keep warm. Repeat with remaining batter, spraying griddle with cooking spray if necessary to prevent sticking.

1 pancake: 145 Calories; 4.0 g Total Fat (2.0 g Mono, 1.1 g Poly, 0.6 g Sat); 20 mg Cholesterol; 23 g Carbohydrate; 2 g Fibre; 4 g Protein; 222 mg Sodium (need new NI)

Tip

To make sour milk, measure 1 Tbsp (15 mL) white vinegar or lemon joiuce into a 1 cup (250 mL) liquid measure. Stir in enough milk to make 1 cup (250 mL). Let stand for 1 minute.

Quinoa Jam-filled Muffins

Makes 12 muffins

Fancy yourself a treasure hunter? Well, you won't have to dig deep to unearth the golden apricot booty stowed in the centre of these not-too-sweet muffins.

1 cup (250 mL) all-purpose flour

1 cup (250 mL) whole wheat flour

3 Tbsp (45 mL) brown sugar, packed

1 1/2 tsp (7 mL) baking powder

3/4 tsp (4 mL) salt

1/8 tsp (0.5 mL) baking soda

1 large egg, fork-beaten

1 1/2 cups (375 mL) cooked quinoa

1 cup (250 mL) buttermilk (or soured milk, see Tip, page 130)

(see next page)

Combine first 6 ingredients in a large bowl. Make a well in the centre.

Combine next 6 ingredients in a small bowl. Add to well in flour mixture. Stir until just moistened. Fill 12 greased muffin cups 2/3 full. Make a small dent in batter with the back of a spoon.

Spoon 1 tsp (5 mL) jam into each dent. Spoon remaining batter over top. Bake in 375°F (190°C) oven for about 25 minutes until firm to the touch. Let stand in pan for 5 minutes. Remove muffins from pan and place on a wire rack to cool.

1 muffin: 239 Calories; 5.2 g Total Fat (1.3 g Mono, 0.4 g Poly, 2.7 g Sat); 26 mg Cholesterol; 45 g Carbohydrate; 3 g Fibre; 5 g Protein; 264 mg Sodium

1 cup (250 mL) raisins

1/4 cup (60 mL) butter (or
hard margarine), melted

1/4 cup (60 mL) maple
syrup

1/4 cup (60 mL) apricot jam

Caribbean Muffins

Makes 12 muffins

Tropical flavours come together to delight your senses—coconut, mango and lime, with crunchy Brazil nuts. Make these when you want to really impress!

1 cup (250 mL) all-purpose flour

1/2 cup (125 mL) whole wheat flour

1/2 cup (125 mL) quinoa flakes

1/4 cup (60 mL) + 2 Tbsp (30 mL) chopped Brazil nuts (or almonds), toasted (see Tip, page 9), *divided*

2 tsp (10 mL) baking powder

1/2 tsp (2 mL) baking soda

1/4 tsp (1 mL) salt

2 x 5.35 oz (150 g) packages of coconut dessert tofu

1/2 cup (125 mL) granulated sugar

1 large egg

1 cup (250 mL) chopped fresh (or frozen) mango

1/2 cup (125 mL) mashed overripe banana (about 1 medium)

1 Tbsp (30 mL) + 1/2 tsp (2 mL) dark (navy) rum, *divided* **(see Tip)**

1 Tbsp (15 mL) lime juice

2 tsp (10 mL) grated lime zest (see Tip, page 98)

(see next page)

Combine both flours, quinoa flakes, 1/4 cup (60 mL) Brazil nuts, baking powder, baking soda and salt in a large bowl. Make a well in the centre.

Beat tofu, granulated sugar and egg in medium bowl until smooth. Stir in next 5 ingredients. Add to well in flour mixture. Stir until just moistened. Fill 12 greased muffin cups 3/4 full. Sprinkle with remaining 2 Tbsp (30 mL) Brazil nuts. Bake in 375°F (190°C) oven for about 25 minutes until a wooden pick inserted in the centre of a muffin comes out clean.

For the glaze, combine last 3 ingredients and remaining 1/2 tsp (2 mL) rum in a small saucepan. Bring to a boil on medium. Heat and stir for about 1 minute until slightly thickened. Spoon over hot muffins. Let stand in pan for 5 minutes before removing to a wire rack to cool.

1 muffin: 200 Calories; 4 g Total Fat (1 g Mono, 1 g Poly, 1.5 g Sat); 20 mg Cholesterol; 35 g Carbohydrate; 2 g Fibre; 4 g Protein; 170 mg Sodium

Tip

You can use rum extract in place of the rum, if you prefer.

1/4 cup (60 mL) brown sugar, packed

1 Tbsp (15 mL) butter (or hard margarine)

2 tsp (10 mL) lime juice

Quinoa Apple Carrot Cake

Makes 1 cake that cuts into 12 wedges

A healthier version of a beloved classic. It looks like your ordinary carrot cake, but quinoa and apple add an appealing dimension of taste.

1 1/2 cups (375 mL) all-purpose flour

1 tsp (5 mL) baking powder

1 tsp (5 mL) ground cinnamon

1/2 tsp (2 mL) baking soda

1/2 tsp (2 mL) salt

3 large eggs, fork-beaten

1 cup (250 mL) brown sugar, packed

2/3 cup (150 mL) canola oil

1 Tbsp (15 mL) finely grated ginger root (or 3/4 tsp, 4 mL, ground ginger)

1 1/2 cups (375 mL) cooked quinoa

1 cup (250 mL) grated carrot

1/2 cup (125 mL) grated peeled cooking apple (such as McIntosh)

2 Tbsp (30 mL) cream cheese, softened

2 Tbsp (30 mL) milk

2 tsp (10 mL) butter (or hard margarine), softened

1/4 tsp (1 mL) vanilla extract

1 1/2 cups (375 mL) icing (confectioner's) sugar

Combine first 5 ingredients in a large bowl. Make a well in the centre.

Combine next 4 ingredients in a medium bowl.

Stir in next 3 ingredients. Add mixture to well and stir until just moistened. Line bottom of a greased 9 inch (23 cm) springform pan with waxed paper (see Tip). Spread batter evenly in pan. Bake in a 325°F (160°C) oven for about 55 minutes until a wooden pick inserted in the centre comes out clean. Run a knife around inside edge of pan to loosen cake. Let stand in pan for 5 minutes. Invert cake onto a wire rack to cool completely. Remove and discard waxed paper from bottom of cake.

For the icing, beat next 4 ingredients in a small bowl until smooth.

Add icing sugar. Beat until smooth. Add more milk if necessary until icing reaches spreading consistency. Spread evenly over top and side of cooled cake.

1 wedge: 406 Calories; 15.7 g Total Fat (8.1 g Mono, 4.2 g Poly, 2.3 g Sat); 51 mg Cholesterol; 61 g Carbohydrate; 2 g Fibre; 6 g Protein; 218 mg Sodium

Tip

If you do not have a springform pan, grease a 9 x 13 inch (23 cm x 33 cm) pan, and bake for 40 to 45 minutes until a wooden spoon inserted in the centre comes out clean.

Banana Bread

Makes 1 loaf that cuts into 16 pieces

Quinoa flakes and Brazil nuts give this bread a nice texture and up the nutrient content and protein. Perfect for an afternoon snack or even a quick breakfast on the go.

1 1/2 cups (375 mL) all-purpose flour

1/2 cup (125 mL) quinoa flakes

1/2 cup (125 mL) sugar

1 Tbsp (15 mL) baking powder

1/2 tsp (2 mL) baking soda

1/2 cup (125 mL) chopped Brazil nuts

1 1/2 cups (375 mL) mashed bananas (about 3)

1 egg

3/4 cup (175 mL) milk

1/4 cup (60 mL) cooking oil

Mix first 6 ingredients together and make a well in the centre.

Mix next 4 ingredients together in a separate bowl. Add to well and mix together until just blended. Spread mixture evenly into a 9 x 5 x 3 inch (23 x 12.5 x 7.5 cm) greased loaf pan. Bake in a 350°F (175°C) oven for 35 to 40 minutes, or until a wooden pick inserted in centre comes out clean. Let stand for 10 minutes before removing to a wire rack to cool.

1 piece: 160 Calories; 6 g Total Fat (3 g Mono, 1.5 g Poly, 1 g Sat); 15 mg Cholesterol; 24 g Carbohydrate; 1 g Fibre; 3 g Protein; 105 mg Sodium

Pumpkin Seed Cookies

Makes about 54 cookies

A small cookie with a big punch! Pumpkin, pumpkin seeds, quinoa, oats and cranberries come together in a cookie that is both delicious and nutritious. You don't have to feel guilty about reaching for one of these little gems.

3/4 cup (175 mL) brown sugar, packed

3/4 cup (175 mL) sugar

1/2 cup (125 mL) butter

1 large egg

1 1/3 cups (325 mL) canned pure pumpkin

1 cup (250 mL) quick cooking rolled oats

1/2 cup (125 mL) quinoa flour

1/2 cup (125 mL) quinoa flakes

1/2 cup (125 mL) all-purpose flour

1 Tbsp (15 mL) baking powder

3/4 tsp (4 mL) ground cinnamon

1/4 tsp (1 mL) ground allspice

1/4 tsp (1 mL) salt

3/4 cup (175 mL) dried cranberries

3/4 cup (175 mL) roasted pumpkin seeds, salted

Beat first 3 ingredients in a large bowl until light and fluffy. Add egg and pumpkin.

Process rolled oats in a blender or food processor until mixture resembles a coarse powder. Transfer to a medium bowl. Stir in next 7 ingredients. Add to pumpkin mixture in 2 additions, mixing well after each addition until no dry flour remains.

Add cranberries and pumpkin seeds. Mix well. Drop about 2 inches (5 cm) apart onto greased cooking sheets, using 1 Tbsp (15 mL) for each. Bake in 375°F (190°C) oven for about 10 minutes until golden brown. Let stand on a cookie sheet for 5 minutes before removing to a wire rack to cool.

1 cookie: 80 Calories; 3.5 g Total Fat (1 g Mono, 0.5 g Poly, 1.5 g Sat); 10 mg Cholesterol; 11 g Carbohydrate; <1g Fibre; 2 g Protein; 60 mg Sodium

Chocolate Quinoa Cookies

Makes 12 cookies

Who knew something so simple could be so good? Rich and chewy, these delicious cookies will disappear quickly with kids and adults alike.

1/4 cup (60 mL) almond butter

3 Tbsp (45 mL) maple syrup

1 Tbsp (15 mL) vanilla extract

1 tsp (5 mL) ground cinnamon

1 cup (250 mL) quinoa sprouts (see page 7)

1/4 cup (60 mL) shredded coconut

1/4 cup (60 mL) chocolate chips

3 Tbsp (45 mL) cocoa powder

Mix almond butter, maple syrup, vanilla and cinnamon in a medium bowl.

Stir in remaining ingredients. Drop, using 1 Tbsp (15 mL) for each, about 2 inches (5 cm) apart onto cookie sheet lined with parchment paper. Bake in 350°F (175°C) oven for 10 to 15 minutes. Transfer cookies to wire racks to cool.

1 cookie: *120 Calories; 6 g Total Fat (0 g Mono, 0 g Poly, 1.5 g Sat); 0 mg Cholesterol; 15 g Carbohydrate; 2 g Fibre; 3 g Protein; 0 mg Sodium*

Seeds 'n' Grains

Makes 13 oz (370 g), about 38 pieces

Do you crave those supermarket sesame snacks? Well, it's a snap to make them at home.

1 cup (250 mL) granulated sugar

1/4 cup (60 mL) water

1/4 cup (60 mL) white corn syrup

1/4 cup (60 mL) amaranth, toasted (see Tip, page 9)

1/4 cup (60 mL) quinoa, toasted (see Tip, page 78)

1/4 cup (60 mL) sesame seeds, toasted (see Tip, page 9)

1/4 tsp (1 mL) salt

Place a baking sheet with sides upside down on your work surface. Place a sheet of parchment (not waxed) paper on bottom of baking sheet. Cut another piece of parchment paper the same size and set aside. Combine first 3 ingredients in a medium heavy saucepan. Heat and stir on medium until sugar is dissolved and mixture starts to boil. Brush side of saucepan with a wet pastry brush to dissolve any sugar crystals. Boil for about 15 minutes, without stirring, until hard crack stage (300° to 310°F, 150° to 154°C, on candy thermometer) or until a small amount dropped into very cold water separates into hard, brittle threads. Remove from heat.

Add remaining 4 ingredients. Mix well. Pour lengthwise along centre of parchment paper. Place second sheet of parchment paper on top. Working quickly, use rolling pin to press grain mixture to about 1/16 inch (1.5 mm) thickness. Be careful not to squeeze hot sugar mixture out sides of parchment paper. Let stand for 2 minutes. Remove top sheet of parchment paper. Let stand until starting to firm. Cut into 1 x 2 inch (2.5 x 5 cm) rectangles. It is easiest to cut the mixture while it is still a little warm.

1 oz (28 g): 106 Calories; 1.6 g Total Fat (0.6 g Mono, 0.7 g Poly, 0.3 g Sat); 0 mg Cholesterol; 23 g Carbohydrate; 1 g Fibre; 1 g Protein; 50 mg Sodium

Seed and Fruit Bars

Makes 12 bars

These bars are sort of like granola bars, only much tastier and healthier than the commercially prepared kind. Wrap them individually and toss one into your bag for a mid-afternoon pick-me-up, or stash a few in your backpack when hiking for a snack along the trail.

3 cups (750 mL) quinoa flakes

1/2 cup (125 mL) raw sunflower seeds

1/3 cup (75 mL) chopped dried cherries

1/3 cup (75 mL) dried cranberries

1/3 cup (75 mL) golden raisins

1 Tbsp (15 mL) flax seed

1 Tbsp (15 mL) sesame seeds

1/3 cup (75 mL) butter

1/2 cup (125 mL) liquid honey

1/4 cup (60 mL) maple syrup

Combine first 7 ingredients in a large bowl.

Combine remaining 3 ingredients in small saucepan. Heat and stir on medium for about 5 minutes until starting to boil. Remove from heat and drizzle over quinoa mixture. Stir until coated. Press into 9 x 13 inch (23 x 33 cm) pan. Bake at 350°F (175°C) for about 15 minutes until golden. Let stand for about 15 minutes to cool slightly. Run knife around inside edge of pan to loosen. Cut into 12 bars while still warm. Let stand on wire rack until cool.

1 bar: 290 Calories; 10 g Total Fat (2 g Mono, 2.5 g Poly, 3.5 g Sat); 15 mg Cholesterol; 44 g Carbohydrate; 4 g Fibre; 7 g Protein; 40 mg Sodium

Chili Fruit Tarts

Makes 12 tarts

A cherry and apple mixture is nestled in a luxurious quinoa pastry. Sweet chili sauce may seem like an odd pairing for the filling, but the combination is truly outstanding.

1/2 cup (125 mL) apple juice

1/3 cup (75 mL) coarsely chopped cherries

1/4 cup (60 mL) quinoa

1/8 tsp (0.5 mL) ground cinnamon

1 1/3 cups (325 mL) chopped peeled cooking apple

1/4 cup (60 mL) brown sugar

2 Tbsp (30 mL) sweet chili sauce

1 Tbsp (15 mL) all-purpose flour

2 tsp (10 mL) lime juice

1 1/2 cups (375 mL) quinoa flour

1 Tbsp (15 mL) sugar

1/2 cup (125 mL) cold butter, cut up

1/3 cup (75 mL) ice water

1 egg

1 Tbsp (15 mL) water

For the filling, pour apple juice into small saucepan and bring to a boil. Remove from heat. Stir in next 3 ingredients and let stand, covered, for about 8 minutes.

Stir in next 5 ingredients.

For the pastry, combine flour and sugar in a medium bowl. Cut in butter until mixture resembles coarse crumbs.

Add ice water 1 Tbsp (15 mL) at a time, stirring with a fork until mixture starts to come together. Do not overmix. Turn pastry out onto a work surface. Shape into a slightly flattened square. Wrap and chill for 30 minutes. Roll out pastry on a lightly floured surface to 12 x 16 inch (30 x 40 cm) rectangle, about 1/8 inch (3 mm) thick. Cut into twelve 4 inch (10 cm) squares. Press squares into bottom and sides of 12 greased muffin cups. Spoon about 2 Tbsp (30 mL) filling into each cup. Fold corner of pastry over filling.

(see next page)

Whisk egg and water in a bowl. Brush tarts with egg mixture. Bake in 375°F (190 °C) for 30 minutes until golden brown. Let stand for 3 minutes. Remove tarts from pan and place on a wire rack to cool.

1 tart: 200 Calories; 9 g Total Fat (2 g Mono, 0 g Poly, 5 g Sat); 40 mg Cholesterol; 26 g Carbohydrate; 3 g Fibre; 3 g Protein; 85 mg Sodium

Chocolate Cake

Makes 1 cake that cuts into 9 pieces

If you are going to give in to your craving for chocolate, you might as well do it in style. This decadent cake is rich and moist, thanks to the addition of quinoa flour.

1 cup (250 mL) water

1 1/2 cups (375 mL) sugar

1/2 cup (125 mL) butter

3 Tbsp (45 mL) + 1/4 cup (60 mL) cocoa, sifted if lumpy, *divided*

1/2 tsp (2 mL) baking soda

1 cup (250 mL) quinoa flour

1/2 cup (125 mL) all-purpose flour

1 Tbsp (15 mL) baking powder

2 eggs

1/4 cup (60 mL) sugar

1/4 cup (60 mL) butter

1/4 cup (60 mL) water

1 1/2 cups (375 mL) icing sugar

Measure first 4 ingredients and 3 Tbsp (45 mL) cocoa into a medium sauce pan. Heat and stir on medium-low until sugar is dissolved. Simmer, without stirring, for 5 minutes. Transfer to a large bowl. Cool slightly.

Add both flours, baking powder and eggs. Beat until smooth. Pour mixture into greased 9 x 9 inch (23 x 23 cm) pan lined with parchment paper. Bake in a 350°F (175°C) oven for about 40 minutes, until wooden pick inserted in centre comes out clean. Let stand in pan for 10 minutes before removing to wire rack to cool.

For the frosting, combine next 3 ingredients in a small saucepan. Heat and stir on medium-low until sugar is dissolved. Remove from heat. Put icing sugar and 1/4 cup (60 mL) cocoa into a medium bowl. Add butter mixture. Stir until smooth. Cover and chill for about 1 hour, stirring occasionally, until thick. Makes 1 cup (250 mL) of frosting. Spread on top of cooled cake.

1 piece: 460 Calories; 18 g Total Fat (4.5 g Mono, 1 g Poly, 10 g Sat); 90 mg Cholesterol; 73 g Carbohydrate; 3 g Fibre; 5 g Protein; 300 mg Sodium

Apple 'n' Spice Crepes

Makes 6 crepes

This dish is free of both gluten and dairy for a delicious dessert that everyone can enjoy together. Garnish with fresh apples for an attractive presentation.

3 large eggs

1 cup (250 mL) quinoa flour

1 cup (250 mL) vanilla soy milk

1/4 cup (60 mL) + 1 Tbsp (15 mL) tapioca starch (or gluten-free cornstarch), *divided*

1 Tbsp (15 mL) cooking oil

1/4 tsp (1 mL) salt, *divided*

6 cups (1.5 mL) sliced peeled cooking apple (such as McIntosh)

1/4 cup (60 mL) brown sugar, packed

1/4 cup (60 mL) golden raisins

1/2 tsp (2 mL) ground cinnamon

1/4 tsp (1 mL) ground ginger

1/8 tsp (0.5 mL) ground nutmeg

1 cup (250 mL) apple juice

For the crepes, combine eggs, soy milk, flour, 1/4 cup (60 mL) tapioca starch, cooking oil and 1/8 tsp (0.5 mL) salt in a blender. Process until smooth. Let stand for 30 minutes. Heat a small non-stick frying pan on medium. Spray with cooking spray. Stir batter. Pour 3 Tbsp (45 mL) batter into pan. Immediately tilt and swirl pan to ensure bottom is covered. Cook for about 1 minute until edges are dry and centre is no longer shiny. Transfer to a plate. Repeat with remaining batter, spraying pan with cooking spray as necessary to prevent sticking. Makes about 12 crepes (see Tip). Fold each crepe into quarters. Arrange crepes, slightly overlapping, on individual serving plates or a large platter.

For the topping, combine next 6 ingredients and remaining 1/8 tsp (0.5 mL) salt in a large frying pan. Cook on medium for about 15 minutes, stirring often, until apples start to soften and release juices.

Stir apple juice into remaining 1 Tbsp (15 mL) tapioca starch in a small bowl until smooth. Add to apple mixture. Heat and stir until boiling and thickened. Makes about 3 1/2 cups (875 mL) topping. Spoon over crepes. Garnish with a sprinkling of cinnamon.

1 crepe: *300 Calories; 7 g Total Fat (2.5 g Mono, 1.5 g Poly, 1 g Sat); 105 mg Cholesterol; 54 g Carbohydrate; 5 g Fibre; 7 g Protein; 210 mg Sodium*

Tip

Crepes can be made in advance and stored in an airtight container in the freezer for up to 1 month, or in the refrigerator for up to 1 day. To reheat, thaw the frozen crepes and stack them on a baking sheet. Cover with foil and bake in a 200°F (95°C) oven until the crepes are warmed through.

Mango Berry Crisp

Makes 6 servings

Fruit crisp with a mango twist! The sweet-tart fruit flavours and crunchy, buttery topping are best served warm.

3 cups (750 mL) frozen mango pieces, thawed

2 cups (500 mL) frozen mixed berries, thawed

2 Tbsp (30 mL) plus 1/3 cup (75 mL) packed brown sugar, *divided*

1 Tbsp (15 mL) plus 1/4 cup (60 mL) quinoa flour, *divided*

1/4 tsp (1 mL) grated lemon zest

1/3 cup (75 mL) butter

3/4 cup (175 mL) quick-cooking rolled oats

1/4 cup (60 mL) quinoa flakes

1/4 tsp (1 mL) vanilla extract

salt to taste

Preheat oven to 425°F (220°C). Combine mango, berries, 2 Tbsp (15 mL) brown sugar, 1 Tbsp (15 mL) flour and lemon zest in a medium bowl. Transfer to a greased 8 x 8 inch (20 x 20 cm) microwave-safe baking dish. Microwave, uncovered, on high (100%) for about 5 minutes until hot. Stir.

Meanwhile, melt butter in a small saucepan on medium. Add oats, quinoa flakes, remaining 1/3 cup (75 mL) brown sugar, remaining 1/4 cup (60 mL) flour, vanilla and salt. Stir until mixture resembles coarse crumbs. Scatter over mango mixture. Bake for about 15 minutes until top is golden and fruit is bubbling.

1 serving: 310 Calories; 12 g Total Fat (3 g Mono, 0.5 g Poly, 7 g Sat); 25 mg Cholesterol; 50 g Carbohydrate; 5 g Fibre; 4 g Protein; 85 mg Sodium

Quinoa Pudding

Makes 6 servings

A traditional comfort food with a twist. Quinoa replaces rice in this rich, creamy pudding, which is equally delicious served warm or cold.

2 cups (500 mL) milk

1 cup (250 mL) 18% cream

1 cup (250 mL) quinoa

1/4 cup (60 mL) granulated sugar

1/2 tsp (2 mL) ground cinnamon

1/4 (1 mL) salt

1 tsp (5 mL) orange zest

2 tsp (10 mL) vanilla extract

1/2 cup (125 mL) dried cranberries

1/2 cup (2 mL) slivered almonds, toasted (see Tip, page 9)

In a heavy saucepan, bring first 7 ingredients to a simmer over medium heat, stirring often.

Reduce heat to low. Cover and simmer, stirring occasionally, for 20 minutes. Stir in vanilla. Cover and simmer, stirring occasionally, for about 5 minutes until quinoa is very tender. Stir in cranberries. Spoon into individual serving dishes. Top with almonds. Serve warm or cold.

1 serving: 320 Calories; 14 g Total Fat (5 g Mono, 2.5 g Poly, 6 g Sat); 30 mg Cholesterol; 38 g Carbohydrate; 3 g Fibre; 11 g Protein; 90 mg Sodium

Index